D1491257

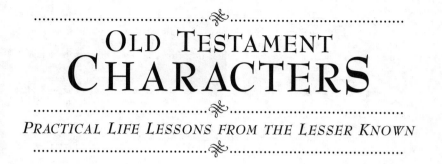

OLD TESTAMENT
CHARACTERS

PRACTICAL LIFE LESSONS FROM THE LESSER KNOWN

Insight for Living Bible Study Guide

From the Bible-Teaching Ministry of

Charles R. Swindoll

The Bible teacher of *Insight for Living*, Charles R. Swindoll has devoted his life to the clear, practical application of God's Word and His grace. A pastor at heart, Chuck has served as senior pastor to congregations in Texas, Massachusetts, and California. He currently leads Stonebriar Community Church in Frisco, Texas, but Chuck's listening audience extends far beyond a local church body. As a leading program in Christian broadcasting, *Insight for Living* airs around the world in major Christian radio markets and to a growing webcast audience, reaching churched and unchurched people groups in a language they can understand. Chuck's extensive writing ministry has also served the body of Christ worldwide, and his leadership as president and now chancellor of Dallas Theological Seminary has helped prepare and equip a new generation for ministry. Chuck and Cynthia, his partner in life and ministry, have four grown children and ten grandchildren.

Based on the original outlines, charts, and transcripts of Charles R. Swindoll's sermons, the study guide text was written by Ken Gire, a graduate of Texas Christian University and Dallas Theological Seminary. In 1991 *Old Testament Characters* was revised by the educational products department, and in 2003 the guide was revised and expanded by the creative ministries department of Insight for Living.

Unless otherwise identified, all Scripture references are from the New American Standard Bible © The Lockman Foundation 1960, 1962, 1963, 1968, 1971, 1972, 1973, 1975, 1977, 1995. Used by permission.

Editor in Chief:
Cynthia Swindoll

Editor and Assistant Writer:
Greg Smith

Study Guide Writers:
Marla Alupoaicei
Ken Gire

Editors:
Maridee Dietzel
Cari Harris
Amy LaFuria

ISBN: 1-57972-575-9
Cover design: Joe Casas
Cover image: *Samson Pulls Down the Pillars* by James Jacques Joseph Tissot
Image Credit: The Jewish Museum, N.Y./Art Resource, N.Y.

CONTENTS

INTRODUCTION

Scriptural character studies never fail to encourage us in our pilgrimage. That's one of the reasons God included snapshots of so many people in His Book. He wants us to see His truth reflected in all these lives—even in the most obscure and unfamiliar individuals.

These Old Testament biographical sketches are designed to help us identify with a few of the ancients. We'll smile and weep, frown and sigh, feel the stinging consequences of sin, and happily rejoice in the victories of various men and women. We will also see ourselves in a new light.

This is all part of the Lord's plan. Our faithful heavenly Father has preserved each life in still portraits for our examination. I encourage you to study each one carefully with me. Stop, look, and listen for those insights that will open new doors of understanding. Don't be afraid to compare. God's Word is a timeless mirror that gives us a true reflection of what pleases Him and what grieves Him.

I am pleased to introduce each one of these people to you. As their lives are unveiled, my prayer is that you will receive helpful perspective and wisdom, which will result in greater stability, a stronger commitment to biblical principles, and a broader awareness of how God works in our lives today.

Chuck Swindoll

Charles R. Swindoll

PUTTING TRUTH
INTO ACTION

Knowledge apart from application falls short of God's desire for His children. He wants us to apply what we learn so that we will change and grow. This study guide was prepared with these goals in mind. As you go through the following pages, we hope your desire to discover biblical truth will grow as your understanding of God's Word increases and that you will be encouraged to apply what you've learned.

To assist you in your study, we've included a section called **Living Insights** at the end of each chapter. These exercises will challenge you to study further and to think of specific ways to put your discoveries into action.

Each Living Insights section is followed by **Questions for Group Discussion**. These thought-provoking questions will help you facilitate discussion of the important concepts and principles in the chapter and apply them to your life.

There are many ways to use this guide — in personal devotions, group studies, discussions with friends and family, and Sunday school classes. And, of course, it's an ideal study aid when you're listening to its corresponding *Insight for Living* radio series.

To benefit most from this study guide, we would encourage you to consider it a spiritual journal. That's why we've included space in the Living Insights for recording your thoughts and discoveries. We hope you'll return to those sections often for review and encouragement as you continue to grow in your walk with Christ.

Insight for Living

OLD TESTAMENT
CHARACTERS

PRACTICAL LIFE LESSONS FROM THE LESSER KNOWN

Chapter 1

SAMSON: A HE-MAN WITH A SHE-WEAKNESS

Judges 13–15

From Greek mythology to Saturday morning cartoons—from Hercules to the He-Man of the Universe—heroes loom immortal in our imaginations. And few heroes cast as long and impressive a shadow as Samson. His able-to-leap-tall-buildings-in-a-single-bound resumé reads like Superman's: killed a lion with his bare hands . . . slaughtered thirty Philistines who had plotted against him . . . defeated a thousand-man band of enemies with the jawbone of a donkey . . . destroyed the city gates at Gaza.

But just as Superman was vulnerable to kryptonite, Samson had a chink in his armor through which his great strength was sapped: when it came to women, he melted before his own passions.

Samson's mother may have been a strong center of gravity in his childhood home, but once he left, Samson entered a misguided orbit that revolved around three women—his bride, a harlot, and Delilah. His desire for these women formed a magnetic field that pulled him off of God's path and onto a collision course that led to his demise.

Samson and His Mother

From a quiet, yet miraculous beginning to a tragic, yet triumphant climax, Samson's life encompasses all the elements of a Shakespearean drama. Act 1 of Samson's life opens in Judges 13. As the curtain rises, a dark backdrop reveals sinful Israel in bondage to the neighboring country of Philistia.

> Now the sons of Israel again did evil in the sight of the Lord, so that the Lord gave them into the hands of the Philistines forty years. (v. 1)

1

Against this dismal historical canvas, a lamp of hope is lit for the nation. Lighting the wick is an angel of the Lord who visits the barren wife of Manoah:

> There was a certain man of Zorah, of the family of the Danites, whose name was Manoah; and his wife was barren and had borne no children. Then the angel of the Lord appeared to the woman and said to her, "Behold now, you are barren and have borne no children, but you shall conceive and give birth to a son. Now therefore, be careful not to drink wine or strong drink, nor eat any unclean thing. For behold, you shall conceive and give birth to a son, and no razor shall come upon his head, for the boy shall be a Nazirite to God from the womb." (vv. 2–5a)

Hope's emerging flame begins to dispel the nation's darkness in the latter portion of verse 5: "and he shall begin to deliver Israel from the hands of the Philistines."

In verses 6–7, the woman tells her husband about the divine encounter. Afterward, Manoah entreats the Lord to have the messenger return (v. 8). Verses 9–23 record this second angelic visitation. A godly, yet somewhat anxious father, Manoah questions the angel concerning the child's upbringing and professional future: "Now when your words come to pass, what shall be the boy's mode of life and his vocation?" (v. 12). Manoah is motivated not by curiosity, but by his commitment to raise the child to be best prepared for his destiny.

This commitment is underscored by the couple's rush to offer a burnt offering to the Lord in reverential submission to His will (v. 19). In a miraculous display, fire shoots up from the altar toward heaven, and the angel of the Lord ascends out of sight (v. 20). Sometime later, a son is indeed born to this godly couple (v. 24). His mother gives him the name *Samson,* derived from the Hebrew word *semes,* meaning "sun." He was most likely named this in anticipation of his powerful strength.[1]

Blessed by the Lord, the boy grows, and the Spirit of the Lord begins to stir in him in a mighty way (v. 25). Upon this act, the curtain falls.

From this part of Samson's life we can glean the first of four principles: *Sensuous children can be born of spiritual parents.* A godly, biblical

---

1. Geoffrey W. Bromiley, gen. ed., *The International Standard Bible Encyclopedia, Volume Four* (Grand Rapids, Mich.: William B. Eerdmans Publishing Co., 1988), see "Samson."

home life is no guarantee against sensuality, as Samson's life will progressively illustrate. He was a child born of prayer . . . whose coming was announced in an angelic appearance . . . was raised by a family that was sensitive and obedient to the Lord . . . was blessed by the Lord . . . and was uniquely visited by the Holy Spirit. But if Samson's life teaches us anything as parents, it demonstrates that even children with a spiritual head start can plunge headlong into carnality.

Samson and His Bride

By the time the curtain rises in Judges 14, many years have passed. Samson is now a virile young man whose hormones boil within him like pent-up steam in a pressure cooker. Unable or unwilling to control his passions, he sees a Philistine woman and becomes obsessed with her.

> Then Samson went down to Timnah and saw a woman in Timnah, one of the daughters of the Philistines. So he came back and told his father and mother, "I saw a woman in Timnah, one of the daughters of the Philistines; now therefore, get her for me as a wife." Then his father and his mother said to him, "Is there no woman among the daughters of your relatives, or among all our people, that you go to take a wife from the uncircumcised Philistines?" But Samson said to his father, "Get her for me, for she looks good to me." (vv. 1–3)

Samson's eyes spur his lust to break the dual reins of his parents' wishes and the Mosaic Law (v. 3; Deut. 7:1–3). Again, in Judges 14:7, as if the Spirit is drawing our attention to the bent in his character, we are informed that "she looked good to Samson."

From this brief episode we gain a second principle: *A sensuous person focuses on the external rather than on the internal.* The first recorded words of Samson are, "I saw a woman." Three times in the passage Samson refers to the Philistine woman in exclusively visual terms. Notice that he does not mention any of her internal qualities. He probably didn't even know what they were!

Just as an attractive, carved wood frame cradles a Rembrandt masterpiece, so our external appearance should frame our internal qualities in a way that highlights them but doesn't overshadow them. When a frame is ornately carved, scrolled, and overlaid with gold leaf, it is easy for our focus to shift from the painting to the frame.

This is precisely why Peter warns: "Your adornment must not be merely external . . . but let it be the hidden person of the heart" (1 Peter 3:3–4). When you look at someone, is your focus on the frame or on the Rembrandt? Do you dwell on the appearance, or do you look past it to the heart (1 Sam. 16:7)?

In spite of Samson's runaway lust, God is still in control of the situation:

> However, his father and mother did not know that it
> was of the Lord, for He was seeking an occasion against
> the Philistines. Now at that time the Philistines were
> ruling over Israel. (Judg. 14:4)

Samson's destiny is to deliver Israel from the Philistines—even in his disobedience. God works through Samson's lust to drive a wedge into the ranks of the Philistines—a wedge so strong that it eventually causes the destruction of Israel's mighty foe.

Verses 5–9 record an incident in Samson's life when "the Spirit of the Lord came upon him mightily" to help him overcome an attacking lion (v. 6). Later, a swarm of bees forms a hive within the lion's carcass, out of which Samson scoops honey for himself. He uses this incident to pose a riddle to the thirty Philistine companions who had accompanied his bride to a seven-day feast. Bets are placed on both sides, and the riddle is set forth:

> "Out of the eater came something to eat,
> And out of the strong came something sweet." (v. 14)

The Philistines are given a time limit of seven days to unravel the riddle. By the fourth day, still stumped, they threaten Samson's bride, getting her to entice him into revealing the answer. After days of pleading and weeping, she finally wheedles the answer out of him and promptly tells it to her countrymen. Just before the deadline, the Philistines answer Samson's riddle:

> So the men of the city said to him on the seventh
> day before the sun went down,
> "What is sweeter than honey?
> And what is stronger than a lion?" (v. 18a)

Realizing he has been duped, Samson's rage starts with a verbal accusation and ends with a violent act.

And he said to them,
  "If you had not plowed with my heifer,
  You would not have found out my riddle."
Then the Spirit of the Lord came upon him mightily, and he went down to Ashkelon and killed thirty
of them and took their spoil and gave the changes of
clothes to those who told the riddle. And his anger
burned, and he went up to his father's house.
(vv. 18b–19)

Hardly in the honeymoon mood, Samson storms away to his
father's house. Left behind, his wife is then given to one of his companions (v. 20). Sometime later, the harvest moon begins to exert a
tidal pull on Samson's libido. Before he knows it, he's at the door to
his wife's room with flowers in hand. (Actually, it was a goat, but
that doesn't translate very romantically into our culture!)

  But after a while, in the time of wheat harvest,
  Samson visited his wife with a young goat, and said,
  "I will go in to my wife in her room." (15:1a)

Enter the father-in-law, who stands at his daughter's door to sand-
bag the flood of Samson's passion:

  But her father did not let him enter. Her father said,
  "I really thought that you hated her intensely; so I
  gave her to your companion. Is not her younger sister more beautiful than she? Please let her be yours
  instead." (vv. 1b–2)

As his thoughts turn quickly from romance to revenge, Samson's
rage rushes to fill the sudden emotional vacancy.

  Samson then said to them, "This time I shall be blame-
  less in regard to the Philistines when I do them harm."
  Samson went and caught three hundred foxes, and
  took torches, and turned the foxes tail to tail and put
  one torch in the middle between two tails. When he
  had set fire to the torches, he released the foxes into
  the standing grain of the Philistines, thus burning up
  both the shocks and the standing grain, along with
  the vineyards and groves. (vv. 3–5)

One act of revenge begets another as the Philistines retaliate by
burning Samson's wife and her father (v. 6). In turn, Samson strikes

5

them ruthlessly with a great slaughter (vv. 7–8). Bound with ropes, Samson is given over to the Philistines by his fearful countrymen (vv. 11–13). Again, however, the Spirit of the Lord comes upon Samson, and he slays a thousand of his captors with the jawbone of a donkey (vv. 14–17).

These dramatic events in Samson's life provide us with our third principle: *The sensuous life brings one anxiety after another.* The denial of Samson's physical gratification led to anger, which, in turn, led to violence and then more violence. The Book of Proverbs wisely observes: "A hot-tempered man abounds in transgression" (29:22). The sensuous life is baited with enticing honey, but honey is always sticky, and the results of partaking of it can be tragic (7:23). Is the bait worth the heartache? Is the snare worth taking that fatal step into transgression? Absolutely not.

Samson and the Harlot

For twenty years Samson ruled as judge over Israel (Judg. 15:20) and apparently ruled righteously and by faith (Heb. 11:32–34). However, we are told in Judges 16:1 that when he went to Gaza, he "saw a harlot there, and went in to her." Little did he realize that this "walk on the wild side" would lead him into a snare that would eventually cost him his life.

This episode brings us to our fourth principle: *Sensuality may be dormant, but it is never dead.* Like embers smoldering beneath the surface of a thought-to-be-extinguished campfire, lust, when fanned in the open air, can fuel a forest fire. And, invariably, someone always gets burned. Scripture tells us:

> For on account of a harlot one is reduced to a loaf
>   of bread,
> And an adulteress hunts for the precious life.
> Can a man take fire in his bosom,
> And his clothes not be burned?
> Or can a man walk on hot coals,
> And his feet not be scorched? (Prov. 6:26–28)

Samson's lustful escapades are also graphic visual reminders of James 1:14–15: "But each one is tempted when he is carried away and enticed by his own lust. Then when lust has conceived, it gives birth to sin; and when sin is accomplished, it brings forth death."

Each snare in this tragic hero's life is tripped by his sensuality. Like the "bird [that] hastens to the snare" (Prov. 7:23), Samson ultimately forfeits his life for failing to avoid the lure of lust.

Living Insights

Samson left his hair uncut because he was a Nazirite. The word *Nazirite* comes from the Hebrew verb *nāzar*, meaning "to separate." The related word *nēzer*, meaning "a diadem," signifies the crowning of a king or queen.[2] Numbers 6:7 says "his separation to God is on his head," alluding to the Nazirite's long, uncut hair, which was considered a beautiful ornament or "crown."

When a person took the Nazirite vow, he or she consecrated himself to God, either for an entire lifetime or for a shorter period of time. In some instances, children's parents dedicated them before birth to be lifelong Nazirites. Samson and Samuel fit this category. John the Baptist and the apostle Paul chose to take Nazirite vows, and Samuel's mother, Hannah, may have as well.

Numbers 6:1–21 records the laws that pertained to Nazirites. Look up the following passages and record the distinctive requirements that God had for these men and women.

6:3–4 _____

_____

6:5 _____

_____

6:6–7 _____

_____

6:8 _____

_____

6:9 _____

_____

2. Merrill F. Unger, *The New Unger's Bible Dictionary* (Chicago, Ill.: Moody Press, 1988), see "Nazirite."

7

6:10–12 _____

_____

6:13–17 _____

_____

6:18–21 _____

_____

What was so sacred and meaningful about the Nazirite vows?

_____

_____

_____

_____

In what ways did Samson break the biblical guidelines listed above?

_____

_____

_____

_____

In what ways are we, as believers, set apart and consecrated to God? How can we demonstrate to others that we're consecrated to the Lord?

_____

_____

_____

_____

_____

Questions for Group Discussion

1. The Nazirites observed certain customs in order to demonstrate tangibly their vows to the Lord. Do your words and actions demonstrate that you belong to God? If so, how? If not, why not?

2. Even more important than the outward acts of obedience were the attitudes of a Nazirite's heart toward God. Take a few moments to examine your heart. Emotionally and spiritually, are you responsive toward God, or do you feel distant from Him?

3. If you feel distant, why do you think this is? How can your friends in your small group help you feel more connected and accountable to the Lord?

4. In which contexts (friendships, family, marriage, parenting, work, school, church, activities) is it easiest for you for demonstrate your faith? In which contexts is it hardest? Why?

5. Samson's lack of self-control, his love of sensual pleasures, and his failure to stay focused on God became his downfall. What messages do we commonly receive from our culture that entice us to follow the same path?

6. How do you guard yourself personally against these sensual messages? How can you and your group members help each other guard against the temptations that you face every day?

Chapter 2

SAMSON: HOW THE MIGHTY ARE FALLEN!

Judges 16:4–31

In Greek mythology, Peleus, king of the Myrmidons, and Thetis, a sea goddess, had a son named Achilles. Achilles enjoyed great honor as the greatest, bravest, and most handsome warrior of Agamemnon's army. One of the tales about his childhood relates how Thetis held her young son by the heel and dipped him in the waters of the river Styx. Through the waters' mythological powers, Achilles became invulnerable—that is, every part except the heel by which he was held. That small portion of his body, untouched by the water, remained vulnerable.

From this story, we get the term "Achilles' heel," which describes our greatest point of vulnerability. It was at just this point that an arrow later struck the near-invincible Achilles and killed him.

We all have our own "Achilles' heels"—points of extreme vulnerability in our walk with God. For some, it's money; for others, it's power or ambition. For Samson, it was sensuality.

Samson's Delilah

When Samson left the harlot of Gaza (Judg. 16:1–3), he fell into the arms of yet another woman—the infamous Delilah. Hebrew scholars assign various meanings to Delilah's name, from "delicate" and "devoted" to "coquettish" and "amorous." Scripture introduces us to her this way:

> After this it came about that he loved a woman in
> the valley of Sorek, whose name was Delilah. (v. 4)

The valley of Sorek was "the place of the choice red grape."[1] Certain foods connote to us worlds of description. For example, beans and cornbread may suggest poverty, while caviar and champagne suggest luxury and extravagance. "The place of the choice red grape"

---

1. Alfred Edersheim, *Old Testament Bible History* (Grand Rapids, Mich.: William B. Eerdmans Publishing Co., 1972), vol. 3, p. 174.

connotes pleasure. The name itself seems to exude the enticing bouquet of sensuality.

Samson roamed through this hedonistic valley, picking the luscious Delilah from the vine to be his next conquest. The irony was that *he*—not Delilah—would end up being conquered. Knowing Samson's weakness for women, the Philistines solicited Delilah's help to discover the secret of his strength.

One author writes,

> [Delilah] was presumably a Philistine, though that is not expressly stated, only that she belonged to the valley of Sorek. She is not spoken of as Samson's wife, though many have understood the account in that way. The text simply says that he loved her (v. 4). The Philistines paid her a very high price for her services: eleven hundred pieces of silver [each]. The account indicates that for mental ability, self-command, and nerve, she was a remarkable woman. Unfortunately, she put her gifts to an evil use by exploiting Samson's love.[2]

The Philistine lords recognized the powerful spell that Delilah's dark beauty had cast on Samson. They recruited her to "work her magic" and discover the secret behind his strength:

> The lords of the Philistines came up to her and said to her, "Entice him, and see where his great strength lies and how we may overpower him that we may bind him to afflict him. Then we will each give you eleven hundred pieces of silver." (v. 5)

The Hebrew word *entice* means "to find an opening"—a point of vulnerability, an Achilles' heel. The same word is used earlier when Samson's wife is threatened by the Philistines: "*Entice* your husband, so that he will tell us the riddle, or we will burn you and your father's house with fire" (14:15, emphasis added).

The word *entice* is also used in James 1:14: "But each one is tempted when he is carried away and *enticed* by his own lust" (emphasis added). Here the Greek word means "luring with bait." It brings to mind a fish nestled quietly in a sheltered place, and a cunning

2. Geoffrey W. Bromiley, gen. ed., *The International Standard Bible Encyclopedia, Volume One* (Grand Rapids, Mich.: William B. Eerdmans Publishing Co., 1988), see "Delilah."

fisherman who has just dropped the bait. Whether artificial or real, the bait is designed to appeal to the nature of the fish—to *entice*. And different fish are enticed by different baits.

For Samson, the enticement is the lure of the "unattainable" woman. Delilah draws him in slowly, but surely, like an unsuspecting fish. Naively, he takes the bait, and fatefully, the hook is set. Follow the progression in Proverbs 7:6–23 to see how Samson ends up on Delilah's stringer.

> For at the window of my house
> I looked out through my lattice,
> And I saw among the naive,
> And discerned among the youths
> A young man lacking sense,
> Passing through the street near her corner;
> And he takes the way to her house. . . .
> And behold, a woman comes to meet him,
> Dressed as a harlot and cunning of heart.
> She is boisterous and rebellious,
> Her feet do not remain at home. . . .
> So she seizes him and kisses him
> And with a brazen face she says to him:
> "I was due to offer peace offerings;
> Today I have paid my vows.
> Therefore I have come out to meet you . . .
> And I have found you.
> I have spread my couch with coverings,
> With colored linens of Egypt.
> I have sprinkled my bed
> With myrrh, aloes and cinnamon.
> Come, let us drink our fill of love until morning;
> Let us delight ourselves with caresses.
> For my husband is not at home,
> He has gone on a long journey. . . ."
> With her many persuasions she entices him;
> With her flattering lips she seduces him.
> Suddenly he follows her
> As an ox goes to the slaughter,
> Or as one in fetters to the discipline of a fool,
> Until an arrow pierces through his liver;

> As a bird hastens to the snare,
> So he does not know that it will cost him his life.

This passage illustrates that there is pleasure in sexual sin—at least for a season—but its grapes are quick to ferment and sour. Like the naive young man in this passage, we all have our weak points. It was Achilles' unprotected heel that proved fatal to the mythological hero, and it was Samson's vulnerability to sexual enticement that led to his demise. Samson's example illustrates that it's important for us to know our strengths, but it is more than essential that we recognize our weaknesses—it literally can be a matter of life and death. When we're aware of our weaknesses and turn them over to the Lord, He can use us more fully (see 2 Cor. 12:9). When our weaknesses are blind spots, however, we're in trouble.

What is your Achilles' heel? Is it lust, greed, ambition, sex, pride, selfishness, drugs, materialism, alcohol, worry, anger? Possibly, like Samson, your area of weakness is a blind spot to you. But you can bet that the people around you see your weaknesses in high definition on the big screen and hear them in surround sound! Certainly the Philistines could see Samson's weakness. Why don't you ask a few friends for a candid film review of your life? Remember that "faithful are the wounds of a friend, but deceitful are the kisses of an enemy" (Prov. 27:6). And be thankful that you're surrounded by friends rather than by Philistines!

Judges 16:6–14 records Delilah's attempts to unravel the mystery of Samson's strength in order to weaken him for the Philistines. In verses 6, 10, and 13, she questions him, and Samson gives answers that progressively gravitate toward the truth: "Bind me with seven fresh cords that have not been dried" (v. 7); "Bind me tightly with new ropes which have not been used" (v. 11); "Weave the seven locks of my hair with the web and fasten it" (v. 13).

Frustrated, Delilah poses a final pointed question to Samson. And his answer leads to his demise.

Samson's Demise

Ironically, the strongest of men is weakened not by soldiers or armies, but by the wiles of one scheming, sensuous woman. Samson could break the ropes and cords that entwined him, but he could not extricate himself from his entanglement with Delilah. Samson's cards, which he had held so close to his chest, are trumped by this persistent woman's final ace: "How can you say 'I love you,' when your heart is not with me?" (v. 15). He folds under pressure in verse 16 and finally reveals his hand in verse 17.

> So he told her all that was in his heart and said to her, "A razor has never come on my head, for I have been a Nazirite to God from my mother's womb. If I am shaved, then my strength will leave me and I will become weak and be like any other man."

Samson's hair was only an outward symbol of his inward commitment to God. Obviously, the latter had eroded to such an extent that the former was no longer sacred to him. In reality, Samson's superhuman strength lay not in his uncut hair, but in the mighty presence of God in his life (v. 20).

The fall of Samson can be traced to two things: (1) he didn't know his weakness, and (2) he didn't know his strength. Mistakenly, Samson doesn't realize that God is the real source of his strength. Instead, he sees only himself (see 15:14–17). Consequently, God allows Samson's strength to be taken from him so that in painful circumstances he will learn that without the omnipotent God, he is impotent.

As he sleeps, his hair is shaved (16:19). When he awakes, he is surrounded not by the presence of the Lord, but by the vengefully cruel Philistines (vv. 20–21). They seize him, gouge out his eyes, shackle him in bronze chains, and force him into the lowest work a slave in prison could do—grind grain while harnessed to a millstone.

Samson had grown to depend on his own strength instead of God's. To teach us to lean on Him and not on false supports, God sometimes removes our crutches—gently, but suddenly and without warning. This is exactly what He did with Samson.

What about you? Are you trusting in something other than God for your safety, your security, or your strength? Are you depending more on your job, your portfolio, your plans, or your bank account than you are on the Lord? If so, keep in mind that God may take away your crutch—not so you will fall, but so you will learn, as Samson did, to lean on Him. Scripture tells us:

> The name of the Lord is a strong tower;
> The righteous runs into it and is safe.
> A rich man's wealth is his strong city,
> And like a high wall in his own imagination.
> (Prov. 18:10–11)

Samson's Death

During Samson's dark experience in the dungeon, God's grace begins to glimmer. Samson's hair starts growing back (v. 22)! And as his hair grows, so does his strength and his relationship with the Lord. Now humbled and completely dependent on God, Samson turns his thoughts and heart back to his Father.

Meanwhile, more than three thousand Philistines have gathered to offer a great sacrifice to the grain god, Dagon, their principal deity (vv. 23–24). For entertainment, the Philistines summon Samson from prison, carousing and making sport of this once-great warrior as he stands between the pillars of the house (vv. 25–27). Humiliated, Samson makes a final request of God:

> Then Samson called to the Lord and said, "O Lord God, please remember me and please strengthen me just this time, O God, that I may at once be avenged of the Philistines for my two eyes." Samson grasped the two middle pillars on which the house rested, and braced himself against them, the one with his right hand and the other with his left. And Samson said, "Let me die with the Philistines!" And he bent with all his might so that the house fell on the lords and all the people who were in it. So the dead whom he killed at his death were more than those whom he killed in his life. (vv. 28–30)

In a final, momentous act of courage and self-denial, Samson fulfills his destiny and begins "to deliver Israel from the hands of the Philistines" (13:5).

A Final Application

With beggar's hands of faith, Samson reaches out to touch the feet of his God: "O Lord God, please remember me. . . ." (16:28). If you're an unbeliever, you can pray with the thief on the cross—"Remember me"—and be assured that you will be with Jesus in paradise (Luke 23:42–43). If you're a believer with a burden, you can pray with Hannah—"Remember me"—and be assured of His compassionate love to help you cope with your difficult circumstances (1 Sam. 1:11–20). If you're a believer who's blown it, you can pray with Samson—"Remember me"—and be assured that God's strength can help you overcome your defeated past (Judg. 16:28–30).

Maybe somewhere along the line you've forgotten God. The tendency is to think that He, too, has forgotten you. But if the very hairs of your head are numbered, how could He forget you? Call to Him, won't you? Whether you're a condemned thief, a burdened Hannah, or a wayward Samson, reach out with hands of faith to touch His feet and heart with the simple prayer—"Remember me."

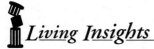 *Living Insights*

Resisting the lure of lust is a tough job—in fact, it's a battle. And that means we need to know our resources, our weapons, and our enemy's strategy. In Proverbs, Solomon passed on a battle plan to his sons. Let's familiarize ourselves with his wise directives.

Spend some time reading Proverbs 5–7, keeping your eye out for four specific topics: (1) descriptions of the harlot, (2) descriptions of the fool who succumbs to her, (3) descriptions of the wise man who turns away, and (4) practical advice on how to avoid the harlot. Record your observations here.

Descriptions of the Harlot

_____

_____

_____

_____

Descriptions of the Fool

_____

_____

_____

_____

Descriptions of the Wise Man

_____

_____

_____

_____

Practical Advice

_____

_____

_____

_____

 Questions for Group Discussion

1. What would you say are your greatest strengths? How do you utilize these strengths in your family, your relationships, your job, your church, and your community?

2. What do you consider your Achilles' heel? How does Satan use this area of weakness to discourage you and try to keep you from growing in your spiritual walk?

3. What do you think you need to do in order to overcome your weaknesses? How can God and the promises you find in His Word help you to improve in these areas?

4. Spiritually, would you describe Samson as a success or a failure? What lessons do you think he learned over the course of his life?

5. Think of some other biblical examples of people who fell prey to lust. How did their sinful choices affect them spiritually, emotionally, and physically? What truths can you glean from their experiences to apply to your own life?

Chapter 3

ABIGAIL:
A WOMAN OF WISDOM

1 Samuel 25

Hollywood thrives on Cinderella stories with happily-ever-after endings. Deep down inside—regardless of how fairy-tale-ish they seem—stories like this thrill us because we have an innate longing for things to work out happily in the end. Our sense of justice causes us to despise Cinderella's ugly, cruel stepsisters and to cheer on the kind, handsome prince as he sweeps Cinderella off her feet. We become wrapped up in the drama because we ourselves are often surrounded by cruel and ugly circumstances. Like Cinderella, we long for some charming, princely circumstance to come along and whisk us away from the drudgery of scrubbing life's dirty floors.

First Samuel 25 contains one such script. The lead actress, Abigail, plays an Academy Award-winning part that any woman would admire.

The Cast

Chapter 25 resembles a three-act play. Following the cast's introductions, we find a description of the *conflict* on which the plot is centered, escalating action that leads to a *climax*, and a *conclusion* that resolves the conflict. In verses 1–3, the three primary cast members are introduced—David, Nabal, and Abigail.

> Then Samuel died; and all Israel gathered together and mourned for him, and buried him at his house in Ramah. And David arose and went down to the wilderness of Paran.
>
> Now there was a man in Maon whose business was in Carmel; and the man was very rich, and he had three thousand sheep and a thousand goats. And it came about while he was shearing his sheep in Carmel (now the man's name was Nabal, and his wife's name was Abigail. And the woman was intelligent and beautiful in appearance, but the man was harsh and evil in his dealings, and he was a Calebite), that David heard in the wilderness that Nabal was shearing his sheep.

The contrast in character between Nabal and Abigail stands out sharply and intensifies the dramatic premise that revolves around the upcoming conflict between David and Nabal.

The Conflict

David and his band of six hundred men looked after the animals of numerous ranchers in the wilderness of Paran, protecting them from thieves and animals of prey. Payment for the service, like gratuities for waiters, was voluntary. No contracts were written; no verbal agreements were made. But it was understood, like the custom of tipping, that at sheepshearing time a rancher was to pay everyone who had protected his animals (see v. 21).

> So David sent ten young men; and David said to the young men, "Go up to Carmel, visit Nabal and greet him in my name; and thus you shall say . . . "'Please give whatever you find at hand to your servants and to your son David.'" (vv. 5–6, 8)

The request was gracious and fair in light of their service and protection (see v. 15). Nabal's miserly, penny-pinching response, however, was far from gracious or fair.

> But Nabal answered David's servants and said, "Who is David? And who is the son of Jesse? There are many servants today who are each breaking away from his master. Shall I then take my bread and my water and my meat that I have slaughtered for my shearers, and give it to men whose origin I do not know?" (vv. 10–11)

Nabal had sheared many sheep, but David would not be one of them. When David heard from his servants how Nabal tried to fleece them out of what was justly due to them, he set out to do a little fleecing of his own.

> David said to his men, "Each of you gird on his sword." So each man girded on his sword. And David also girded on his sword, and about four hundred men went up behind David while two hundred stayed with the baggage. (v. 13)

The Climax

Meanwhile, back at the ranch, Nabal's wife, Abigail, was alerted to the situation:

> But one of the young men told Abigail, Nabal's wife, saying, "Behold, David sent messengers from the wilderness to greet our master, and he scorned them. Yet the men were very good to us, and we were not insulted, nor did we miss anything as long as we went about with them, while we were in the fields. They were a wall to us both by night and by day, all the time we were with them tending the sheep. Now therefore, know and consider what you should do, for evil is plotted against our master and against all his household; and he is such a worthless man that no one can speak to him." (vv. 14–17)

Had Abigail reacted like any ordinary woman trapped in an unhappy, mismatched marriage, she might have been tempted to sit back and allow David's vengeance to run its course. After all, Nabal's death would release her from her relationship with this miserable man. But Abigail is no ordinary woman. Selflessly, she steps in to make peace:

> Then Abigail hurried and took two hundred loaves of bread and two jugs of wine and five sheep already prepared and five measures of roasted grain and a hundred clusters of raisins and two hundred cakes of figs, and loaded them on donkeys. She said to her young men, "Go on before me; behold, I am coming after you." But she did not tell her husband Nabal. It came about as she was riding on her donkey and coming down by the hidden part of the mountain, that behold, David and his men were coming down toward her; so she met them. (vv. 18–20)

The meeting could have been a fiery clash, but Abigail's humility and honesty douse David's wrath like water on a campfire.

> When Abigail saw David, she hurried and dismounted from her donkey, and fell on her face before David and bowed herself to the ground. She fell at his feet and said, "On me alone, my lord, be the

blame. And please let your maidservant speak to you, and listen to the words of your maidservant. Please do not let my lord pay attention to this worthless man, Nabal, for as his name is, so is he. Nabal is his name and folly is with him; but I your maidservant did not see the young men of my lord whom you sent.

"Now therefore, my lord, as the Lord lives, and as your soul lives, since the Lord has restrained you from shedding blood, and from avenging yourself by your own hand, now then let your enemies and those who seek evil against my lord, be as Nabal. Now let this gift which your maidservant has brought to my lord be given to the young men who accompany my lord. Please forgive the transgression of your maidservant; for the Lord will certainly make for my lord an enduring house, because my lord is fighting the battles of the Lord, and evil will not be found in you all your days." (vv. 23–28)

In verse 28, Abigail's view of God as the sovereign source of blessing shapes her appeal in verses 29–31. Her plea softens David's heart and turns his mind back toward the things of God.

Then David said to Abigail, "Blessed be the Lord God of Israel, who sent you this day to meet me, and blessed be your discernment, and blessed be you, who have kept me this day from bloodshed and from avenging myself by my own hand. Nevertheless, as the Lord God of Israel lives, who has restrained me from harming you, unless you had come quickly to meet me, surely there would not have been left to Nabal until the morning light as much as one male." So David received from her hand what she had brought him and said to her, "Go up to your house in peace. See, I have listened to you and granted your request." (vv. 32–35)

Abigail had come to intercede as a peacemaker and ends up leaving with David's assurance: "Go up to your house in peace" (v. 35). The blessing bestowed on her by God for being a peacemaker far exceeds her wildest imaginings (compare Matt. 5:9).

The Conclusion

Abigail returns home to find her husband holding a self-indulgent feast where he had become "very drunk" (v. 36). She waits until the next morning to tell Nabal of her encounter with David. Once informed, he is seized with fear and falls into a coma (v. 37). God intervenes ten days later: "The Lord struck Nabal, and he died" (v. 38). However, the drama doesn't end on a dismal note, but in fairy-tale fashion.

> When David heard that Nabal was dead, he said, "Blessed be the Lord, who has pleaded the cause of my reproach from the hand of Nabal and has kept back His servant from evil. The Lord has also returned the evildoing of Nabal on his own head." Then David sent a proposal to Abigail, to take her as his wife. . . . Then Abigail quickly arose, and rode on a donkey, with her five maidens who attended her; and she followed the messengers of David and became his wife. (vv. 39, 42)

Thus we end our story, as the happy couple rides off into the sunset.

Final Reviews

But what is the critic's review? What can be learned from this moving drama? We can glean at least five vital relationship principles.

First, from verse 3: *Differences between husbands and wives do not mean that the marriage cannot continue.* Differences bring not only negative conflicts, but positive challenges. Sparks may fly on occasion, but as iron sharpens iron, so one person can sharpen another (Prov. 27:17).

Second, from verses 17–18: *The wife's primary role is to support her husband.* She's called to love him, encourage him, and to meet his needs as well as she can. It is God's responsibility to make her husband a godly, wise, responsible leader.

Third, from verses 19 and 36: *Silence and good timing are two of the most effective ways to handle a strained relationship* (see also 1 Peter 3:1–2). Abigail, with her submissive, gentle, and quiet spirit, knew instinctively what to say and when to say it.

Fourth, from verse 25: *There is a difference between harsh criticism and honest realism in relating to your mate.* The difference lies in your motive. Are you criticizing your spouse simply to try to change his or her habits, or are you speaking the truth in love to help your mate grow in his or her relationship with Christ?

Fifth, from verse 39: *God honors the wife who honors her husband* (see also 1 Peter 3:5–6). Abigail must have suffered enormously in her marriage to foolish Nabal. But in this case, God stepped in, and Abigail was relieved of that terrible strain. In some cases, God doesn't remove us from a difficult marriage or relationship, but He gives us grace to bear the load.

As the curtain falls, we feel like giving the drama a standing ovation. Justice is done. Wrong is either righted or forgiven. A bad marriage ends through God's sovereign touch, and a new one begins with God's blessing. Cinderella meets her Prince Charming, and we feel assured that they will live happily ever after.

Living Insights

As we study the life of Abigail, it's clear that she was a godly woman. She possessed many of the traits that other biblical writers mention when praising qualities of womanhood.

Read through 1 Samuel 25 again and write down your observations about Abigail's characteristics.

_____

_____

_____

_____

Now, read each of the following passages and note what they say about godly women.

Genesis 2:18–25

_____

_____

_____

_____

Proverbs 31:10–31

_____

_____

_____

_____

Ephesians 5

_____

_____

_____

_____

1 Peter 3

_____

_____

_____

_____

Which of Abigail's character traits can you pinpoint in these Scripture passages? List them below.

_____

_____

_____

_____

In Abigail, we find a rare blend of feminine ingenuity and wifely support. It's a winning combination! If you're a wife, which of the characteristics listed above do you most reflect? In which areas do you need to grow?

_____

_____

_____

_____

If you're a husband, which characteristics of a godly woman does your wife reflect? How can you show your appreciation and encourage her spiritual growth?

_____

_____

_____

_____

Take some time now to pray about your relationships with your spouse, your family, friends, coworkers, and others with whom you may interact on a daily basis. Ask God to season your thoughts with grace, your words with kindness, and your actions with love.

Questions for Group Discussion

1. How would you characterize Abigail's words and actions in this biblical account? If she had reacted differently, how do you think the situation would have turned out?

2. Compare and contrast David and Nabal. How do you think God viewed each of them? How were their attitudes and responses different?

3. If you could step into the drama of any event in Scripture, what would it be, and why?

4. What relationship principles can we glean from the story of David, Abigail, and Nabal? How do you think the marriage of David and Abigail differed from that of Nabal and Abigail?

5. With regard to your role in your own marriage or relationships, with which of these three main characters do you best identify? Why?

Chapter 4

ABSALOM: THE REBEL PRINCE CHARMING

2 Samuel 13–18

From "All My Children" to "The Bold and the Beautiful" to classics like "Dallas" and "General Hospital," soap operas teem with stories of power, greed, lust, adultery, and intrigue. Nothing is sacred; no one is safe. Everything and everyone is up for grabs. It's survival of the fittest, on both a personal and a corporate level. In these jungles of tangled family relationships, brother is pitted against brother, sister against sister, wife against husband, father against son. Such is the stuff of television melodrama.

Part of the lure of these shows is that their settings don't exist only in the writer's imagination. Soap opera plots are taken from real life, based on real relationships with real people. Then, the scriptwriters mix in plenty of mystery, sex, and murder plots to spice them up.

We find a family feud of soap-opera proportions in 2 Samuel, where a son's bitterness against his father breaks its fetters and runs loose, unrestrained. This bitterness festers, growing into hatred and, finally, utter rebellion. And, since this young man happens to be the king's son, not only is the king endangered, but the kingdom itself is in harm's way.

The story centers on the life and family of David, the greatest king in Israel's history. This royal family lived in a fishbowl, and their drama became nightly viewing for the entire nation. Sex, ambition, murder, political intrigue, cover-ups, power struggles—they had enough plots, subplots, and counterplots to fill seasons of programming on every major network. In this episode, the main stars are Absalom and David.

Absalom's Home

The family tree from which Absalom sprang resembled an overgrown orchard. David had seven wives in Hebron and numerous wives and concubines in Jerusalem. With his wives alone, David fathered at least twenty sons and one daughter, Tamar. With boughs weighed down so heavily, it's no surprise that some of the offspring would fall from the tree and spoil.

Such was the case with Absalom; however, the finger of blame cannot be pointed solely at the young rebel. Because of his father's polygamy, Absalom grew up in a fragmented home, without a sense of how a God-centered Jewish family should operate. Also, Absalom saw sin and inconsistency in his father's life, and this, no doubt, affected him tremendously.

The passing of time seems to cover a multitude of sins for history's heroes. Now we look upon David with awe and admiration. The headlines we remember are: "Shepherd Boy Slays Giant" . . . "War Hero Becomes King" . . . "David: A Man after God's Own Heart." David did win many victories, and he enjoyed a close, blessed relationship with God for most of his life. But David, too, was human, and he made mistakes. At home, Absalom got the inside scoop on his father David's life.

Absalom's family was divided by rivalry, and the halls of the palace were rife with intrigue and gossip during his formative years. Absalom lived through his father's involvement with Bathsheba, his attempt to cover up his sexual sin, and his arrangement of the murder of Uriah. David's string of sinful choices makes Watergate look like a child's game of hide-and-seek.

Let's get personal for a moment. What story is your family reading about your life? Are they buying the journalistic hype at the newsstand, or are they doing some investigative reporting of their own behind the scenes? What do you think they're uncovering—honesty or hypocrisy? Will they find submission to God or selfish attitudes and sinful actions?

You can expend a lot of energy—as David did—in covering up your sin, or you can channel that energy into living your life with integrity so that a cover-up isn't necessary. Remember, the true story of your life—front page, sports page, comics—is being read by impressionable eyes. And those eyes find it difficult to forgive and forget.

Absalom's Bitterness

Professionally, David was enmeshed in the affairs of state and diplomacy. Domestically, he had so many wives, concubines, and children that the time he had at home was spread far too thin to be effective. It is no surprise, then, that as we jump from chapter 3 to chapter 13—a leap of twenty years—no mention is made of Absalom. He's simply overlooked by the biblical writer, which undoubtedly was what happened in his relationship with David. He was simply overlooked by a father who was either too busy or too tired for too long.

It's easy to overlook little things, especially when it comes to your children. You may be too tired to play catch with your son or take your daughter to the park when you get home from work, so you overlook the fact that your child has waited all day for you to come home. Perhaps you're so busy with work taken home from the office or with domestic chores that you fail to read your kids a bedtime story or tuck them into bed. You may be so enmeshed in the newspaper or your favorite TV program that you overlook the fact that your child is struggling with a confusing homework assignment and really needs your help.

In *Poor Richard's Almanac*, Benjamin Franklin illustrated the importance of taking care of details and how disastrous it can be when they are overlooked:

> For want of a nail the shoe was lost; for want of a shoe the horse was lost; and for want of a horse the rider was lost; being overtaken and slain by the enemy, all for want of care about a horseshoe nail.[1]

Just as neglecting the little things can destroy your relationships, taking care to attend to the little details can build your relationships and keep them strong and healthy.

Amnon's Violation of Tamar

Second Samuel chapter 13 describes an incident that further deepens Absalom's bitterness toward his father. David's oldest son, Amnon, had fallen in love with his half sister, Tamar, who was Absalom's sister. By following the wicked scheme of his friend Jonadab, Amnon lured Tamar into his room, and then he raped her (vv. 1–14).

As soon as his sexual appetite had been temporarily sated, Amnon's feelings toward Tamar changed. Scripture says that "the hatred with which he hated her was greater than the love with which he had loved her" (v. 15). Tamar fled, hurt and humiliated, to stay with Absalom (v. 20).

King David heard of Amnon's crime and became "very angry" (v. 21), but we have no record that he issued any reprimand. David's failure to punish Amnon's crime is of enormous consequence, since the Mosaic Law plainly stated this offense was an abomination and

---

1. Benjamin Franklin, as quoted in *Five Thousand Quotations for All Occasions*, ed. Lewis C. Henry (Garden City, N.Y.: Doubleday and Co., 1945), p. 28.

the offender must be cut off from the nation of Israel (see Lev. 18). But David wanted to keep this unpleasant incident out of the papers, so he swept the dirt under the family rug. Undoubtedly, David's refusal to punish Amnon added further to Tamar's feelings of desolation and fueled the fires of Absalom's burning anger toward his father.

Absalom's Revenge against Amnon

After two years of letting his revenge simmer on the back burner, Absalom turns up the heat in a plot to murder Amnon. With David's approval, Absalom arranges for Amnon to take the grand tour of his sheepshearing enterprise in Baal-hazor. However, under this façade of friendliness, Absalom brews a covert plot that he delegates to his servants: "See now, when Amnon's heart is merry with wine, and when I say to you, 'Strike Amnon,' then put him to death. Do not fear; have not I myself commanded you? Be courageous and be valiant" (2 Sam. 13:28).

As the plot unfolds like the scenes of a Hollywood murder mystery, Amnon is killed, and Absalom flees for three years to hide with his grandfather, Talmai, king of Geshur. Eventually, Absalom is recalled to Jerusalem and resettles, but he is not reconciled to his father (14:1–24).

Absalom's Conspiracy

The motive and method of Absalom's conspiracy against David bubbles to the surface during the two years that he resides, estranged from his father, in Jerusalem.

Absalom's Motive

For two years, Absalom has been allowed to live in Jerusalem but not permitted to see his father (vv. 21–24). Angrily, Absalom forces Joab, one of David's men, to negotiate a meeting between him and his father: "Now therefore, let me see the king's face, and if there is iniquity in me, let him put me to death" (v. 32).

A meeting is arranged in which Absalom prostrates himself before the king, and then the king kisses him. The scene has all the external staging of a reconciliation, but something is missing. Both men seem to be playing out contrived roles—acting out parts rather than reacting with genuine emotion. It is clear that Absalom no longer looks to David as a father with whom to be reconciled, but as a foe to be reckoned with.

Absalom's Method

Verses 25–26 give us a glimpse of Absalom's physical appearance and his growing popularity:

> Now in all Israel was no one as handsome as Absalom, so highly praised; from the sole of his foot to the crown of his head there was no defect in him. When he cut the hair of his head (and it was at the end of every year that he cut it, for it was heavy on him so he cut it), he weighed the hair of his head at 200 shekels by the king's weight. (2 Sam. 14:25–26)

With his personal charm and political charisma (14:25; 15:1–5), Absalom "[steals] away the hearts of the men of Israel" (v. 6). Cunningly, he uses his influence to construct his own cabinet of men who had defected from David's circle of leadership (v. 12). The groundswell conspiracy ripples through the palace right under David's nose.

Suddenly caught in the vortex of a coup d'état, David and his servants flee the palace (vv. 13–14). As a personal affront to his father, Absalom enters the royal harem to have sex with his father's wives and concubines on the same porch where David had relations with Bathsheba (16:20–23).

Absalom's Death

As David organized an army to recapture Jerusalem, he ordered his men to deal gently with Absalom. Meanwhile, Absalom, riding under an overgrown oak tree, got his long hair entangled in its branches and was left hanging helplessly in midair. Finding Absalom in the tree, Joab ignored David's previous plea for leniency and drove three spears into this rebel son's heart.

In spite of the fact that this threat had been removed, David grieved greatly over the loss of his son. Wounds of regret remained in his mind and heart, goading his conscience. Hearing the news of Absalom's death, David responded with deep sorrow and remorse:

> The king was deeply moved and went up to the chamber over the gate and wept. And thus he said as he walked, "O my son Absalom, my son, my son Absalom! Would I had died instead of you, O Absalom, my son, my son!" (18:33)

Some Concluding Applications

The story of Absalom's relationship with his father is a tragic one, but we can learn some valuable lessons through their painful mistakes.

First: *An unhappy home breeds unbalanced children.* We reap what we sow. When good crops aren't planted, tares of indulgence will grow in their place, making for a backbreaking harvest. Are you cultivating a happy home, or are you too tired, too busy, or unwilling to sow the right kind of seed (see Prov. 24:30–34)? Remember, if you sow nothing, you can expect to reap only weeds. And you'll harm the lives of those entrusted to you, as well.

Second: *An undisciplined family breeds insecurity and resentment.* We have no record of David ever disciplining his children for their many wrongs. Children need enforced boundaries to give them a sense of security. They need a degree of freedom, but only within the secure grounds provided by well-constructed fences. When children cut holes in the fences you have erected, and you fail to hold them accountable for their actions, they question your love for them (see Prov. 13:24). Eventually, this leads to resentment and, ultimately, to rebellion.

Third: *An unreconciled relationship breeds sores that never heal.* Even the death of the resented person can't stanch ill feelings. Unreconciled hurt has a way of reaching out from the grave and wagging its bony finger at the one still living. Say the words you need to say now, while you still have time. Forgiveness—not geographical separation or even death—is the only way to restore estranged relationships. Paul's advice here is timely:

> Let all bitterness and wrath and anger and clamor and slander be put away from you, along with all malice. Be kind to one another, tender-hearted, forgiving each other, just as God in Christ also has forgiven you. (Eph. 4:31–32)

Living Insights

An old proverb states, "Like father, like son." In some ways, Absalom followed in his father's footsteps, but he failed to reflect many of the positive attributes that made David "a man after God's own heart."

Some timely and practical lessons emerge from this study of family relationships. Let's spend time on each one as we grab biblical truths and plug them into our personal lives.

First, we learned that an unhappy home breeds unbalanced children. Why is this true? How have you observed this in people's lives?

_____

_____

_____

_____

What are some definite ways you can contribute to making your home happy? Name a few.

_____

_____

_____

_____

Next, we learned that an undisciplined family breeds insecurity and resentment. Why do you think this is the case? What specific examples of this dynamic come to mind for you?

_____

_____

_____

_____

Do luxury and leisure have priority over godly principles in your home? If so, how can you better prioritize God's Word and His principles?

_____

_____

_____

_____

How were discipline and punishment handled in your childhood home? How are they handled in your current family situation?

_____

_____

_____

_____

If you had to pinpoint a weak area in your discipline of your children, what would it be? During this next week, how can you work on that weakness?

_____

_____

_____

_____

Lastly, we learned that an unreconciled relationship breeds sores that never heal. Are you haunted by any unreconciled relationships? If so, how can you work on finding healing in those areas?

_____

_____

_____

_____

Have any of your relationships been suffering from neglect? If so, list three ways you can work toward resolving this problem this week. Then, take a few moments to pray for the strength and motivation to follow through with your plans.

_____

_____

_____

_____

_____

Questions for Group Discussion

1. How did David's attitudes and actions influence Absalom? What was positive about David's influence? What was negative?

2. What lessons can we learn about parenting from the example of David and Absalom?

3. In what ways have your parents, mentors, and other leaders had a positive influence on you? What have you learned from your relationships with these people?

4. If you could go back in time and change certain aspects of your relationship with your parents or other influential people in your life, what would you change?

5. What three attributes do you think are most important for a parent to display? What does Scripture have to say about these characteristics?

6. What three attributes do you feel are most important for parents to cultivate in their children? What biblical passages can you find to support your ideas?

Chapter 5

REHOBOAM:
THE RECKLESS PHONY
1 Kings 11–14

With a dazzling array of movie stars, expensive sets, and special effects, the movie industry makes its living by manufacturing illusions—making a façade look real. The words "Lights . . . camera . . . action!" draw us into an artificial world contrived to create a sense of reality. But true reality is not recorded on reels of film and shown in theaters. True reality happens off-camera, behind the scenes.

When we sit in a darkened theater, watching a movie producer's finished product, it's difficult to spot the tricks that make the fantastic special effects possible. However, when we go behind the scenes—off-camera—it's easy to spot what's phony and what's real. In this chapter, we're going to examine the life of a man named Rehoboam to see what was real and what was phony in his life.

The Roots of Rehoboam's Phoniness

You don't have to trace Rehoboam's genealogical roots very far to find the source of his duplicitous life. Rehoboam's father was Solomon, and his mother was Naamah, a distinguished Ammonite woman.[1] Undoubtedly, Rehoboam had read his father's Song of Songs, which extolled the sanctity and beauty of the marriage relationship.

However, Solomon's seven hundred wives and three hundred concubines surely revealed a discrepancy between what he wrote and how he lived his private life (1 Kings 11:3). To please his foreign wives, Solomon built temples to false gods in and around Jerusalem (vv. 5–8). International marriages commonly required the recognition of foreign deities, and Solomon's were no exception. As a result,

---

1. The Ammonites were descendants of Lot's youngest daughter. She lived in Sodom, where sensual cults and the pagan gods Molech and Milcom had their roots. Worship of these deities involved abominable sexual practices and the sacrifice of children in a furnace of fire. "Excavations in Palestine have uncovered piles of ashes and remains of infant skeletons in cemeteries around heathen altars, pointing to the widespread practice of this cruel abomination." Merrill F. Unger, *Archaeology and the Old Testament* (Grand Rapids, Mich.: Zondervan Publishing House, 1970), p. 279.

these wives "turned his heart away after other gods" (v. 4). Again, Rehoboam saw in his father a dual standard: confessing one God, yet tolerating the influential presence of many foreign gods.

Finally, though he was raised on his father's Proverbs, which stressed wisdom and self-discipline, Rehoboam saw Solomon living a self-indulgent, extravagant lifestyle. (Solomon gave an autobiographical account of his escapades in the book of Ecclesiastes.) When Solomon died, Rehoboam succeeded him at the age of forty-one (v. 43; 14:21). As we will see, his first decision as head of state revealed his two-sided character.

The Examples of Rehoboam's Phoniness

Four incidents in Rehoboam's reign strip the veneer of righteousness that overlaid his life and reveal the cheap, splintered plywood of wickedness. For forty-one years, Rehoboam had lived in his father's shadow, where he learned to play a rehearsed role for the public eye. But all the while, he was nurturing a secret life of self-indulgence.

The Incident regarding Taxation

After Rehoboam took the throne, the people came to him with a request:

> "Your father made our yoke hard; now therefore lighten the hard service of your father and his heavy yoke which he put on us, and we will serve you." (12:4)

Rehoboam sent the people away for three days in order to take this matter under advisement:

> King Rehoboam consulted with the elders who had served his father Solomon while he was still alive, saying, "How do you counsel me to answer this people?" Then they spoke to him, saying, "If you will be a servant to this people today, and will serve them and grant them their petition, and speak good words to them, then they will be your servants forever." (vv. 6–7)

Although Rehoboam went through the motions of seeking counsel from his father's veteran advisers, he rejected their advice and turned to his peers:

> So he said to them, "What counsel do you give that we may answer this people who have spoken to me,

saying, 'Lighten the yoke which your father put on us'?" The young men who grew up with him spoke to him, saying, "Thus you shall say to this people who spoke to you, saying, 'Your father made our yoke heavy, now you make it lighter for us!' But you shall speak to them, 'My little finger is thicker than my father's loins! Whereas my father loaded you with a heavy yoke, I will add to your yoke; my father disciplined you with whips, but I will discipline you with scorpions.'"[2] (vv. 9–11)

Verse 15 states that "the king did not listen to the people." Deep down inside, Rehoboam had no intention of giving ear to the needs of the people. As a result, civil war ensued (vv. 16–24). The ten tribes of the north revolted and established a separate nation under the name Israel, making Jeroboam, a leader of the northern tribes, their king. Rehoboam was left with only two tribes, Judah and Benjamin, which formed the nation of Judah.

The Incident regarding Civil War

Through a man named Shemaiah, God told Rehoboam not to fight against his relatives in the northern kingdom:

"'Thus says the Lord, "You shall not go up or fight against your relatives; return every man to his house, for this thing is from Me."' So they listened to the words of the Lord and returned from going against Jeroboam. (2 Chron. 11:4)

On camera, Rehoboam appears obedient. But off-camera, he actually beefs up his country's defenses for war:

Rehoboam lived in Jerusalem and built cities for defense in Judah. Thus he built Bethlehem, Etam, Tekoa, Beth-zur, Soco, Adullam, Gath, Mareshah, Ziph, Adoraim, Lachish, Azekah, Zorah, Aijalon and Hebron, which are fortified cities in Judah and in Benjamin. He also strengthened the fortresses and put officers in them and stores of food, oil and wine. He put shields

---

2. The "scorpion" referred to here was a lash that had a single handle with nine to twelve leather straps embedded with pieces of bone or metal. The whip had a handle and only a single leather strap.

and spears in every city and strengthened them greatly. So he held Judah and Benjamin. (vv. 5–12)

Rehoboam spent vast amounts of time, money, and resources to fortify Judah for war. This was hardly a picture of a king who obeyed and trusted God!

The Incident regarding the Capital City

On the surface, Jerusalem looked as if it were the city of the Lord. But, in reality, its people followed the pagan customs of Naamah, Rehoboam's Ammonite mother:

> Now Rehoboam the son of Solomon reigned in Judah. Rehoboam was forty-one years old when he became king, and he reigned seventeen years in Jerusalem, the city which the Lord had chosen from all the tribes of Israel to put His name there. And his mother's name was Naamah the Ammonitess. Judah did evil in the sight of the Lord, and they provoked Him to jealousy more than all that their fathers had done, with the sins which they committed. For they also built for themselves high places and sacred pillars and Asherim on every high hill and beneath every luxuriant tree. There were also male cult prostitutes in the land. They did according to all the abominations of the nations which the Lord dispossessed before the sons of Israel. (1 Kings 14:21–24)

When Solomon brought his pagan wives into the city, he erected altars and effigies to their gods. Apparently, Naamah's influence exceeded that of his other wives. The sensuality and human sacrifice that accompanied her form of worship brought abominable practices to Jerusalem. On the surface, Jerusalem bore the Lord's name; it was His city. In reality, however, the city seemed more like a whitewashed tomb, full of death and decay.

The Incident regarding Solomon's Shields

Because of Rehoboam's unfaithfulness to Him, God led the king of Egypt, Shishak, against Jerusalem. This resulted in the pillage of both the Lord's house and the king's palace. Following the plunder, Rehoboam's character again shows through his shallow façade.

So Shishak king of Egypt came up against Jerusalem, and took the treasures of the house of the Lord and the treasures of the king's palace. He took everything; he even took the golden shields which Solomon had made. Then King Rehoboam made shields of bronze in their place and committed them to the care of the commanders of the guard who guarded the door of the king's house. As often as the king entered the house of the Lord, the guards came and carried them and then brought them back into the guards' room. (2 Chron. 12:9–11)

First Kings 10 catalogs the vast array of opulent treasures that Solomon had displayed in his palace. Regarding the shields, he had made "200 large shields of beaten gold, using 600 shekels of gold on each large shield. He made 300 shields of beaten gold, using three minas of gold on each shield" (vv. 16–17).

In hopes that the public wouldn't discover the theft, Rehoboam cleverly arranged for shields to be made out of bronze to replace the gold ones. He worked surreptitiously behind the scenes to conceal the loss, and with the aid of his "special effects department," managed to make the phony bronze substitutes seem like the real thing. To enhance the illusion, he kept the shields from close public view.

A Brief Summary

The Scriptures show us four areas of hypocrisy in Rehoboam's life. He sought others' counsel, but he never really listened to the people. He said he would not fight, but behind the scenes he was fortifying his cities for battle. He lived in a city that was meant to declare the name of the Lord, but he filled it with pagan gods. Finally, he sought to cover up the loss of the stolen gold shields by replacing them with stand-ins made of bronze. In these four scenes we see Rehoboam as a consummate actor, skilled at performances aimed to please the public eye.

Personal Application

The word hypocrite comes from the Greek word hupokrites, which describes a character on the ancient Greek stage who wore a mask as he performed. It's easy to live a theatrical, on-camera existence like Rehoboam, while our off-camera, behind-the-scenes life is full of self-indulgence and deception. We tend to forget that, while we may fool others for a while, we can't fool God. One of His biblical names, *El Shaddai*, means, "the One who sees." The Lord sees past our flimsy masks and straight into our hearts.

Jesus had little tolerance for those who wore masks of deception. He spoke surprisingly harsh words to those who led others astray through false teaching:

> "Woe to you, scribes and Pharisees, hypocrites! For you are like whitewashed tombs which on the outside appear beautiful, but inside they are full of dead men's bones and all uncleanness. So you, too, outwardly appear righteous to men, but inwardly you are full of hypocrisy and lawlessness." (Matt. 23:27–28)

If you're living an on-stage, off-stage double life, remember that in the balcony sits the One whose Word pierces "as far as the division of soul and spirit, of both joints and marrow, and [is] able to judge the thoughts and intentions of the heart. And there is no creature hidden from His sight, but all things are open and laid bare to [His] eyes" (Heb. 4:12–13).

Living Insights

Rehoboam had the outward appearance of having it all together. But a closer look reveals that inside, it was all falling apart.

Why do you think Rehoboam was disobedient? What negative influences in his life contributed to his turning away from God?

_____

_____

_____

_____

In what ways are you tempted to put on masks physically, emotionally, and spiritually?

_____

_____

_____

_____

_____

_____

In what areas of your life do you struggle most to be real and let your true colors show? Why do you think this is?

_____

_____

_____

_____

_____

Instead of feeling free to be ourselves, we often put on masks because we're afraid of being vulnerable with others. We've been hurt before, and we don't want to open ourselves up to be hurt again. The influences of the world tend to make us forget that God created each and every one of us as a unique and beautiful person in His own image.

What positive attributes do you possess—your appearance, character, personality, and giftedness—that make others want to get to know you? Currently, are you highlighting these characteristics or hiding them?

_____

_____

_____

_____

_____

Do you feel that you have to wear a mask around certain individuals? If so, what steps can you take to let them get to know more of the real you?

_____

_____

_____

_____

Questions for Group Discussion

1. How do you see phoniness displayed in the world around you? What impact does this have on you?

2. In what ways do we tend to wear masks, and why? What outward and inward pressures cause us to hide our real selves?

3. What unique, positive character qualities has God given you? How do you use these to serve Him?

4. Instead of masking who you are, how can you highlight your God-given qualities and personality characteristics when interacting with others?

5. In which areas do you struggle to "just be yourself"? Why?

6. How can you make others feel comfortable being themselves around you? In what ways can you communicate God's love, acceptance, and grace to them?

Chapter 6

NAAMAN AND GEHAZI: CHARACTERS IN CONTRAST

2 Kings 5

The literary term *poetic justice* was first introduced in England by Thomas Rymer in 1678. It denotes that the characters in a drama reap the harvest of what they sow—for the virtuous, reward; for the wicked, punishment. This principle emerges in Nahum Tate's 1681 revision of Shakespeare's tragic work *King Lear*. In his revision, Tate deletes the character of the Fool and tacks on a happy ending. The villains die and the heroes live. Lear is restored to his throne, and Cordelia weds Edgar.

In 2 Kings 5, a similar drama unfolds that forever changes the course of the lives of two men, Naaman and Gehazi. The first was a leper; the second, a servant of God's prophet Elisha. In an example of poetic justice, a surprising change transpires in the lives of both men. The leper becomes a servant of God; the servant, in turn, becomes a leper.

As the curtain rises on this drama, we'll be able to see Naaman and Gehazi with front-row clarity. We'll see that both of their faces are shadowed with unbelief, which, in Naaman, manifests itself as pride and, in Gehazi, as greed.

Naaman

Descriptions of Naaman

In the opening credits, Naaman is described in glowing terms:

> Now Naaman, captain of the army of the king of Aram, was a great man with his master, and highly respected, because by him the Lord had given victory to Aram. The man was also a valiant warrior, but he was a leper. (2 Kings 5:1)

Naaman was a high-ranking officer in the Syrian army. His war record was impressive: he was instrumental in bringing peace to the land. His personal references were impeccable: "a great man with his master, and highly respected." And not only was he a great military leader, he was also a "valiant warrior" himself—something like a highly respected player-coach. However, one physical ailment dogged Naaman's every footstep: he was a leper.

Leprosy, in biblical times, was a dreaded skin disease. Those who had this disfiguring, communicable ailment—at least in Israel—were outcasts of society. They were often banished to live in isolated colonies, ostracized by the community (see Lev. 13, especially vv. 45–46). Although Syrian social regulations were not as stringent as those in Israel, the diseased skin of a leper was a stigma that shadowed the person throughout his or her life. A person could be declared "cleansed" of leprosy by a priest, but the disease had no known medical cure (Lev. 14).

Events Leading to Naaman's Cure

Even before Naaman's conversion, God was at work stringing together a chain of events that would lead to the cure of his leprosy, "because by him the Lord had given victory" (2 Kings 5:1). In verse 2, we find a small but indispensable link in this chain: a little Hebrew girl.

> Now the Arameans had gone out in bands and had taken captive a little girl from the land of Israel; and she waited on Naaman's wife. She said to her mistress, "I wish that my master were with the prophet who is in Samaria! Then he would cure him of his leprosy." (vv. 2–3)

This child was used mightily by God to set Naaman on a life-changing course toward healing. The next link in God's chain of events is a bigger one—Naaman's master, the king of Aram.

> Naaman went in and told his master, saying, "Thus and thus spoke the girl who is from the land of Israel." Then the king of Aram said, "Go now, and I will send a letter to the king of Israel." He departed and took with him ten talents of silver and six thousand shekels of gold and ten changes of clothes. (vv. 4–5)

Notice that Naaman thinks like an unbeliever. The first thing that comes to his mind is, "I'll give him money. I'll buy my cure!" So, with his designer garments, his bags laden with gold, and his letter of introduction, Naaman sets off with the wind of optimism in his sails.

> He brought the letter to the king of Israel, say-
> ing, "And now as this letter comes to you, behold, I
> have sent Naaman my servant to you, that you may
> cure him of his leprosy." When the king of Israel read
> the letter, he tore his clothes and said, "Am I God,
> to kill and to make alive, that this man is sending
> word to me to cure a man of his leprosy? But consider
> now, and see how he is seeking a quarrel against me."
> (vv. 6–7)

This superhuman demand made by the king of Aram causes the
king of Israel to tear his robes in frustration. He asks pointedly, "Am
I God?" Upon further reflection, the king wonders if the request
might be some ploy to create an incident between the two kingdoms.
Fortunately for the king, however, the matter reaches Elisha's ears
and is immediately delegated to him.

> It happened when Elisha the man of God heard
> that the king of Israel had torn his clothes, that he
> sent word to the king, saying, "Why have you torn
> your clothes? Now let him come to me, and he shall
> know that there is a prophet in Israel." (v. 8)

Naaman wastes no time beating a direct path to the prophet's door:

> So Naaman came with his horses and his chariots and
> stood at the doorway of the house of Elisha. Elisha
> sent a messenger to him, saying, "Go and wash in the
> Jordan seven times, and your flesh will be restored to
> you and you will be clean." (vv. 9–10)[1]

Once the entourage reaches Elisha's house, Naaman is greeted in
a manner that seems completely inhospitable and humiliating. First,
he is not invited in, but is left to stand in Elisha's doorway. Second,
Elisha doesn't come to greet him, but sends his messenger instead.
Third, the prescription the messenger brings hardly fills the bill of
what Naaman had expected from so great a prophet as Elisha. For a
man who had been accustomed to buying everything he wanted, this
strange prescription was a hard pill to swallow.

Try to envision the emotional backdrop. Naaman is a man of
great status, more used to giving orders than taking them, used to
being able to buy whatever he wants. He has traveled a long way,

---

1. Elisha's prescription is reminiscent of Leviticus 14:1–8, minus some ceremonial detail.

only to endure an incredulous reception by Israel's king. Then he travels farther to the home of Elisha, whom he may have considered simply "some foreign religious fanatic." To his chagrin, Naaman is greeted with humiliation instead of hospitality.

Standing at the doorway with his entourage looking on, Naaman receives an enigmatic order from Elisha's servant. And, as if it weren't bad enough for a Syrian to come to a Jew's land, Naaman was expected to dip himself seven times in the muddy Jordan river. Understanding the background and Naaman's pride, his reply is predictable:

> But Naaman was furious and went away and said, "Behold, I thought, 'He will surely come out to me and stand and call on the name of the Lord his God, and wave his hand over the place and cure the leper.' Are not Abanah and Pharpar, the rivers of Damascus, better than all the waters of Israel? Could I not wash in them and be clean?" So he turned and went away in a rage. (vv. 11–12)

Then, just as Naaman threatens to break the chain, another link holds in place the events leading to his cure.

> Then his servants came near and spoke to him and said, "My father, had the prophet told you to do some great thing, would you not have done it? How much more then, when he says to you, 'Wash, and be clean'?" (v. 13)

In spite of his rage, Naaman realizes that the servants' reasoning is right and reacts more rationally.

> So he went down and dipped himself seven times in the Jordan, according to the word of the man of God; and his flesh was restored like the flesh of a little child and he was clean. (v. 14)

An Observation about Naaman

In Naaman's defense, we can't overlook the fact that he listened to the advice of those under him—the little servant girl (vv. 2–3), Elisha's servant (v. 10), and his own servants (v. 13). God sometimes works in mysterious ways to bring about His will. He speaks through His Word (Heb. 4:12), but He also spoke out of a whirlwind (Job 38:1). He spoke through the prophets (Heb. 1:1), but He also spoke through Balaam's donkey (Num. 22:28).

It appears, then, that the only way to hear all that God has to say to us is to develop a listening ear, a teachable spirit, and an open heart. Proverbs instructs us that "in abundance of counselors there is victory" (11:14). Like some of the Old Testament prophets, those counselors can occasionally come in strange garb—a sunset, a psalm, a sparrow, even a servant.

How are your ears? Have you been in for a hearing test lately—or should we say a *listening* test? Try listening to and learning from a little child, as Naaman did. If you can pass this test, God is beginning to train your ears to hear His footsteps . . . soft, but certain, amid the noisy traffic of everyday life.

Gehazi

Verses 15–19 form a literary bridge by which Naaman and Gehazi are brought together. Thrilled about his cure from his dreaded disease, Naaman rushes to thank Elisha and makes a genuine profession of faith: "Behold now, I know that there is no God in all the earth, but in Israel" (v. 15). Then Naaman urges Elisha to accept a present of gratitude. Upon Elisha's refusal, the cured leper urges the prophet again to receive a gift from his hand.

Meanwhile, standing in the shadows, Elisha's servant Gehazi overhears this volley of offers and refusals. You can almost hear the dollar signs ringing in his head as he tabulates the profit that his master is willingly choosing to give up.

> But Gehazi, the servant of Elisha the man of God, thought, "Behold, my master has spared this Naaman the Aramean, by not receiving from his hands what he brought. As the Lord lives, I will run after him and take something from him." (v. 20)

Seizing an opportunity for financial gain, Gehazi slips out the back door to catch up with Naaman:

> So Gehazi pursued Naaman. When Naaman saw one running after him, he came down from the chariot to meet him and said, "Is all well?" (v. 21)

At this point, Gehazi's imagination starts to run wild, and he bursts forth with a stream of lies:

> He said, "All is well. My master has sent me, saying, 'Behold, just now two young men of the sons of the

47

prophets have come to me from the hill country of Ephraim. Please give them a talent of silver and two changes of clothes.'" Naaman said, "Be pleased to take two talents." And he urged him, and bound two talents of silver in two bags with two changes of clothes and gave them to two of his servants; and they carried them before him. (vv. 22–23)

Gehazi's first lie: "My master has sent me." His second lie: "My master has sent me, *saying*" (emphasis added). He attributes this lie to Elisha's lips. His third lie: "Two young men of the sons of the prophets have come" to stay, and money is needed for their lodging. Gehazi returns to Elisha's house, where he covertly stashes the coins and the clothes. Although he hasn't been caught with his hand in the cookie jar, Gehazi has crumbs all over his red face.

When he came to the hill, he took them from their hand and deposited them in the house, and he sent the men away, and they departed. But he went in and stood before his master. And Elisha said to him, "Where have you been, Gehazi?" And he said, "Your servant went nowhere." (vv. 24–25)

Here we find Gehazi's fourth lie: "Your servant went nowhere." You may have heard the saying, "Never say never." But one "never" that seems appropriate is this: Never, never lie to a prophet! Of all the people in the world most likely to see through a scam and straight into the heart of a person, it's a prophet. Listen to the penetrating questions that pierce through Gehazi's flimsy roof of lies. Then you'll hear Elisha's scathing indictment:

Then he said to him, "Did not my heart go with you, when the man turned from his chariot to meet you? Is it a time to receive money and to receive clothes and olive groves and vineyards and sheep and oxen and male and female servants? Therefore, the leprosy of Naaman shall cling to you and to your descendants forever." So he went out from his presence a leper as white as snow. (vv. 26–27)

An Ironic Ending

The literary term *irony* refers to a situation that embodies the reverse of what is expected. It's ironic that King Arthur's Round Table was destroyed by Lancelot, the very man who helped build it. And it's ironic that Naaman, the Syrian, came away from Elisha cleansed, while Gehazi, the Jew who lived as a servant in Elisha's own house, came away cursed (see Luke 4:27). It's ironic, too, that Naaman, the leper (2 Kings 5:1), became a servant (v. 17), and Gehazi, the servant (v. 20), became a leper (v. 27). In a downpour of poetic justice, Naaman's healing became Gehazi's leprous curse. The truth about Gehazi leaked through his roof of thatched lies to expose his greed and drench it in God's sudden and torrential judgment.

If your life were made into a play, would the main character's flaws be visible like Naaman's leprosy, or would they be hidden like Gehazi's greed? Would the main character listen to the advice of servants like Naaman did, or would he attempt to evade the words of his master like Gehazi did? Has your main character made a public profession of faith—like Naaman's washing in the Jordan—or is there a private world of hidden sin thatched with lies? These are questions we all must come to grips with if we want our lives to have joyful, happy endings.

Living Insights

It would be so easy if, as in the old western movies, the good guys all wore white hats and the bad guys all wore black ones. But life is not usually so neat and tidy. The truth is, everyone is a little bit of a hero—and a little bit of a villain. Those of us who have a relationship with Jesus Christ have become new creations (2 Corinthians 5:17). We possess His goodness and righteousness and the power of the Holy Spirit within us. However, we're still susceptible to making mistakes and committing sins. Satan still whispers words of deceit into our ears to lure us into disobeying God's commands.

What characteristics do you share with Naaman?

_____

_____

_____

What characteristics do you share with Gehazi?

_____

_____

_____

How would you describe Elisha? What was important about his role in this story?

_____

_____

_____

How does Satan try to deceive you in your daily life? To what lures (greed, lust, doubt, and so on) are you most susceptible?

_____

_____

_____

_____

Read Ephesians 6:10–17. How can you arm yourself against Satan's schemes?

_____

_____

_____

_____

Questions for Group Discussion

1. In what ways did Naaman change throughout this story? What did this indicate about him spiritually?

2. Describe Gehazi. How did his actions reflect his inner character? How did his circumstances change by the end of the story?

3. What did you learn about Elisha's character from this chapter? Were you surprised by any of his words or actions? If so, which ones?

4. In what ways was the power of God demonstrated in the lives of these men?

5. What important personal lessons can you glean from this chapter?

Chapter 7

JABEZ: DISADVANTAGED BUT NOT DISQUALIFIED

1 Chronicles 4:9–10

Thousands of the world's best athletes compete in the Olympic Games. Each Olympian's body has been carefully sculpted and fine-tuned to guarantee optimum performance in that individual's event. Marathon runners must be able to withstand incredible physical strain for over twenty-six miles, so they spend their time training their muscles and increasing their endurance. Swimmers must be prepared to propel themselves through the water quickly, powerfully, and efficiently. Gymnasts must be strong, graceful, and versatile enough to perform well on several apparatuses.

The athletes who make it to the Olympics have what it takes to win. They're performing at their peak, with most showing no signs of any type of weakness. But this is not the case for most of us who are running the race of life.

The Old Testament introduces us to Jabez, who was born into difficult circumstances but refused to let that handicap hamper his performance. Jabez appears briefly on the scriptural playing field, goes for the gold, and then drops out of sight, never to be mentioned again. He doesn't make it into the "Faith Hall of Fame" in Hebrews 11, and his name may not appear on many Bible Trivia cards, but his faith challenges us, his positive attitude encourages us, and praying his poignant prayer can change our lives.

A Glance at Jabez

Don't blink, or you'll miss it! Rising out of the dust of 1 Chronicles is a two-verse oasis where you'll catch a brief glimpse of Jabez and his prayer:

> Jabez was more honorable than his brothers, and his mother named him Jabez saying, "Because I bore him with pain." Now Jabez called on the God of Israel, saying, "Oh that You would bless me indeed and enlarge my border, and that Your hand might be with me, and that You would keep me from harm that it

may not pain me!" And God granted him what he requested. (1 Chron. 4:9–10)

His Name

The verse tells us that Jabez's mother "bore him with pain," so she chose to give him the name *Jabez*, which means "pain" in Hebrew. His name could literally be rendered "He causes (or will cause) pain." Not exactly the start of a promising life, is it?

Bruce Wilkinson, author of the best-selling book *The Prayer of Jabez*, writes:

> All babies arrive with a certain amount of pain, but something about Jabez's birth went beyond the usual—so much so that his mother chose to memorialize it in her son's name. Why? The pregnancy or the delivery may have been traumatic. Perhaps the baby was born breech. Or perhaps the mother's pain was emotional—maybe the child's father abandoned her during the pregnancy; maybe he had died; maybe the family had fallen into such financial straits that the prospect of another mouth to feed brought only fear and worry. . . .
>
> Yet by far the heaviest burden of Jabez's name was how it defined his future. In Bible times, a man and his name were so intimately related that "to cut off the name" of an individual amounted to the same thing as killing him. . . . A name that meant "pain" didn't bode well for Jabez's future.[1]

Why would a loving mother give her son such a depressing moniker? Most likely, Jabez's mother named him "Pain" to reveal the hardship into which he was born. Jabez's family must have viewed his name as salt in an open wound—a daily reminder of their tough situation.

Author and Bible teacher Beth Moore notes that the word *pain* is translated *idol* in other Old Testament contexts. She writes:

> In the story of Jabez a blatant association occurs to me. In my opinion his mother made an idol of the pain associated with his birth. I wonder how many of us have also made an idol of our past pain. Not only did

1. Excerpted from *The Prayer of Jabez* by Bruce Wilkinson © 2000 by Ovation Foundation, Inc. Used by permission of Multnomah Publishers, Inc., pp. 20–21.

she bow down to it, she also inflicted the same sentence on Jabez—until one day when he decided maybe his God was bigger than his name. Bigger than his pain.[2]

We can't be certain what kind of hardship or difficulty Jabez was born into. But we do know that throughout his life, he wore the equivalent of a nametag reading, "Hello! My name is Pain."

His Reputation

As his name suggests, Jabez had to endure pain before he could ultimately triumph over it. But, incredibly, he overcame his lowly beginning and rose above his situation to find himself distinguished and favored among his brothers. His story demonstrates that incredible blessings may await even those who seem to have the fewest possibilities. Pastor Charles Haddon Spurgeon wrote:

> It will sometimes happen that where there is the most sorrow in the antecedents, there will be the most pleasure in the sequel. As the furious storm gives place to the clear sunshine, so the night of weeping precedes the morning of joy. Sorrow the harbinger; gladness the prince it ushers in. . . . More honourable than his brethren was the child whom his mother bore with sorrow. . . . The honour [Jabez] enjoyed would not have been worth having if it had not been vigorously contested and equitably won.[3]

His Faith

From his prayer in verse 10, we discover that Jabez believed in God and followed Him. Instead of just telling us about Jabez's faith, the writer illustrates it by opening a window through which we can view Jabez praying his humble, fervent prayer. We read, "Now Jabez called on the God of Israel" (1 Chron. 4:10). He offered a prayer of petition to God, for his hope was in the Lord.

His Prayer

In his prayer in verse 10, Jabez asks four things of God. First, he asks, *"Bless me indeed."* Jabez prays with God-sanctioned vision, asking

2. Beth Moore, *Believing God* (online Bible study, LifeWay Church Resources, 2002), p. 162, available at www.lifeway.com/believinggod/, accessed on November 17, 2003.

3. Charles H. Spurgeon, *The Treasury of the Bible* (Grand Rapids, Mich.: Zondervan Publishing House, 1968), vol. 2, p. 1.

God not merely to bless him, but to bless him *indeed*. This last little word carries great weight in the Hebrew language. Jabez wants more than just to finish the race; he wants to *win*. So he pleads for God to pour out His supernatural favor, goodness, and power on his life. Bruce Wilkinson writes,

> Notice a radical aspect of Jabez's request for blessing: *He left it entirely up to God to decide what the blessings would be and where, when, and how Jabez would receive them.* This kind of radical trust in God's good intentions toward us has nothing in common with the popular gospel that you should ask God for a Cadillac, a six-figure income, or some other material sign that you have found a way to cash in on your connection with Him. Instead, the Jabez blessing focuses like a laser on our wanting for ourselves nothing more and nothing less than what God wants for us.[4]

Second, Jabez asks, *"Enlarge my border."* With God-sanctioned ambition, Jabez begs God for increase. He refuses to fill a small space; he wants God to expand his opportunities for service. He desires more influence, more responsibilities, and more opportunities to make a mark for the God of Israel.

How can we ask for enlarged borders in our own lives? Wilkinson writes:

> When Christian executives ask me, "Is it right for me to ask God for more business?" my response is, "Absolutely!" If you're doing your business God's way, it's not only right to ask for more, but He is waiting for you to ask. Your business is the territory God has entrusted to you. He wants you to accept it as a significant opportunity to touch individual lives, the business community, and the larger world for His glory. . . .
>
> Suppose Jabez had been a wife and a mother. Then the prayer might have gone: "Lord, add to my family, favor my key relationships, multiply for Your glory the influence of my household." Your home is the single most powerful arena on earth to change a life for God.[5]

4. Excerpted from *The Prayer of Jabez* by Bruce Wilkinson © 2000 by Ovation Foundation, Inc. Used by permission of Multnomah Publishers, Inc., p. 24.

5. Excerpted from *The Prayer of Jabez* by Bruce Wilkinson © 2000 by Ovation Foundation, Inc. Used by permission of Multnomah Publishers, Inc., pp. 31–32.

Third, Jabez requests that *"Your hand might be with me."* He understood that when God enlarged his borders, he would need even more desperately to be led by His hand. So Jabez asks for the Lord's guidance. He's not on a power trip; he simply asks for big blessings and big opportunities in ministry, and he willingly places his trust in a big God. Wilkinson continues:

> As God's chosen, blessed sons and daughters, we are expected to attempt something large enough that failure is guaranteed . . . unless God steps in. Take a minute to prayerfully try to comprehend how contrary that truth is to everything you would humanly choose:
>
> - It goes against common sense.
> - It contradicts your previous life experience.
> - It seems to disregard your feelings, training, and need for security.
> - It sets you up to look like a fool and a loser.
>
> Yet it is God's plan for His most-honored servants.
> I'll admit, big-screen heroes don't seem to put any stock in dependence—but you and I were made for it. Dependence upon God makes heroes of ordinary people like Jabez and you and me.[6]

Fourth, Jabez pleads, *"Keep me from harm that it may not pain me!"* Finally, Jabez asks for God-sanctioned protection. In choosing to use the word *pain*, Jabez draws our attention once more to his name, which he links to his nature. He asks the Lord for protection against his own propensity to sin and against the curse that has been imposed upon him by his name. It's as if Jabez is saying, "Let me not experience the grief that my name implies, and that my sins may well produce."[7] He prays for God to save him from his pessimistic past. Jabez is weary of his life of anguish. He wants a fresh start, and he knows Whom to go to for help.

One commentator describes what may have motivated Jabez to offer such a meaningful and heartfelt prayer:

> The prayer of his, . . . in the form of a vow (Gen. 28:20), seems to have been uttered when he was

---

6. Excerpted from *The Prayer of Jabez* by Bruce Wilkinson © 2000 by Ovation Foundation, Inc. Used by permission of Multnomah Publishers, Inc., pp. 47–48.

7. Robert Jamieson, A. R. Fausset, and David Brown, *A Commentary on the Old and New Testaments* (Grand Rapids, Mich.: William B. Eerdmans Publishing Co., 1984), vol. 1, p. 459.

entering on an important or critical service, for the successful execution of which he placed confidence neither on his own nor his people's prowess, but looked anxiously for the aid and blessing of God.[8]

His Answer

The best part of this glimpse of Jabez is that "God granted him what he requested." Everything he asked for, he received (compare Matt. 7:7; John 15:16; James 4:2b). It's no wonder, then, that he was distinguished among his brothers.

A Glance at Ourselves

This short, crisp historical sketch stimulates healthy self-evaluation. It raises three questions that everyone ought to answer. First, *What is my name?* If God were to name you by your nature, what would He name you? Criticism? Shortsightedness? Stubbornness? Or Faithfulness, Kindness, or Generosity?

Second, *Where am I spiritually?* Are you content to stay within your small, self-imposed boundaries, afraid to venture past your borders? Or are you ready to buckle your seatbelt and take an adventurous roller-coaster ride into the great unknown to see what God has in store for you? Are you prepared to have your sphere of influence enlarged? *Radically* enlarged?

Third, *What am I asking of God?* Jabez asked big things of God, and he received them. This poem by the famous missionary Amy Carmichael reflects the same humble attitude that Jabez displayed:

> From prayer that asks that I may be
> Sheltered from winds that beat on Thee,
> From fearing when I should aspire,
> From faltering when I should climb higher,
> From silken self, O captain, free
> Thy soldier who would follow Thee.
>
> From subtle love of softening things,
> From easy choices, weakenings,
> Not thus are spirits fortified,
> Not this way went the Crucified,
> From all that dims Thy Calvary,
> O Lamb of God, deliver me.

8. Jamieson, Fausset, and Brown, *A Commentary on the Old and New Testaments*, vol. 1, p. 459.

Give me the love that leads the way,
The faith that nothing can dismay,
The hope no disappointments tire,
The passion that will burn like fire,
Let me not sink to be a clod:
Make me Thy fuel, Flame of God.[9]

Humility. Love. Faith. Hope. Passion. The desire to be used up for God's purposes. Jabez displayed all of these characteristics and more as he offered himself for God's service. As a result, instead of remaining a hapless victim of an unfortunate name and painful circumstances, Jabez became a victor. He won God's blessing!

The Last Lap

Only the most elite athletes qualify to compete in the Olympic Games. Thankfully, however, the Special Olympics were created for those who have the desire to train and compete, but also have special physical needs.

In these games, the equipment used for every event includes wheelchairs, leg braces, and catheters. Some contestants wear Nikes; some, shoes of two different sizes; others have no feet at all. But in the Special Olympics, all the participants have these things in common: a winning smile, the desire to compete, and the courage to overcome physical obstacles that few of us could imagine.

Face it—in some ways, like Jabez, we were all born with some type of disadvantage. The question is, will you let your disadvantages disqualify you, or will you get out on the track and compete? Will you trust God to get you to the finish line? Every race, whether it's a 5K or a marathon, starts with the first step. God is calling you to take that step today—to stop simply "faith talking" and start "faith walking."

9. Amy Carmichael, "Make Me Thy Fuel" from *Toward Jerusalem* Copyright © 1936 The Dohnavur Fellowship, published by CLC Publications, Fort Washington, Pa., p. 94.

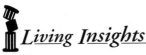

Living Insights

Too often we tend to pat ourselves on the back, thinking that because we aren't complaining about our circumstances, we've achieved spiritual contentment. We're good at using this "façade of contentment" to mask our spiritual laziness. But there's a difference between an attitude that says, "I'm fine right where I am" and one that says, "I'm happy here, but if God has something more for me to do, then I will gladly do it." The former is passivity; the latter, true contentment.

Look up the following passages on contentment and paraphrase both.

Philippians 4:11b

_____

_____

_____

1 Timothy 6:6–8

_____

_____

_____

In which areas of your life do you feel content? In which areas do you struggle with contentment?

_____

_____

_____

_____

Do you feel that you sometimes settle for less than God's best in your life? If so, in which areas?

_____

_____

_____

Why do you think people tend to settle for less than what God wants for them?

_____

_____

_____

_____

In what ways does the Lord want to help you expand your ministry borders and exert a greater influence on others in your life?

_____

_____

_____

_____

Questions for Group Discussion

1. How do you think it affected Jabez to grow up with the name *Pain?* In what ways can pain become an idol or a stumbling block in our lives?

2. If you know the origin and meaning of your name, share it with the group. What is significant about your name? Were you named after anyone? If so, whom?

3. If you could pick a name to best describe your personality and nature, what would it be? What made you pick this name?

4. What disadvantages have you struggled with during your life? In what ways do they affect you emotionally, spiritually, and physically?

5. How did God enable Jabez to turn his disadvantage into blessing? What was so surprising about Jabez's prayer?

6. Write out a short prayer modeled after the prayer of Jabez. In it, ask God to turn your disadvantages into blessings—blessings that will expand God's kingdom, edify others, and enrich your own life.

Chapter 8

UZZIAH: THE KING WHO BECAME A LEPER

2 Chronicles 26

Tombstones—granite tongues of ashen gray—stand row after row in cemeteries like soldiers at attention. Epitaphs—chiseled testimonies to past lives—mutely face the sun, rain, wind, and snow, calling out to the generations that remain. Epitaphs can range anywhere from the trite to the tragic. They can vary in tone from the whimsical "I told you I was sick!" to the poetic:

> The body of
> Benjamin Franklin, printer,
> (Like the cover of an old book,
> Its contents worn out,
> And stript of its lettering and gilding)
> Lies here, food for worms!
> Yet the work itself shall not be lost,
> For it will, as he believed, appear once more,
> In a new
> And more beautiful edition,
> Corrected and amended
> By its Author![1]

As we enter the cemetery of Old Testament characters, we come across the grave of a man of great accomplishment: Uzziah, king of Israel. Suddenly, however, we are struck by an overwhelming incongruity. Where we might have expected an elaborate memorial, we find only a small, simple grave marker. Where we should have seen an eloquent verse chiseled in stone, we read only these words etched on his marker: "He is a leper." Let's read on to discover how a man of Uzziah's monumental achievements came to be remembered so matter-of-factly.

---

1. Benjamin Franklin, as quoted in *The Oxford Book of American Literary Anecdotes*, ed. Donald Hall (New York, N.Y.: Oxford University Press, 1981), p. 13.

Uzziah as a Youth

After Solomon's death, the reins of the kingdom fell into the hands of his son—the greedy, power-hungry Rehoboam, who spurred his people to anger with sharp tax increases. Bucking his rule, the ten northern tribes seceded to form an independent nation under a man named Jeroboam. Consequently, Rehoboam was left to rule the two remaining tribes that he corralled to form Judah, the southern kingdom.

The tenth king down the line from Rehoboam was Uzziah, who ruled for fifty-two years, from 792–739 B.C. His should have been a path of godliness and prosperity, paved by his parents' influence.

> And all the people of Judah took Uzziah, who was sixteen years old, and made him king in the place of his father Amaziah. He built Eloth and restored it to Judah after the king slept with his fathers. Uzziah was sixteen years old when he became king, and he reigned fifty-two years in Jerusalem; and his mother's name was Jechiliah of Jerusalem. (2 Chron. 26:1–3)

We learn from 2 Chronicles 25:2 that Uzziah's father, Amaziah, "did right in the sight of the Lord." His father's example provided the path on which Uzziah was to walk. However, the second part of the verse, "yet not with a whole heart," unearths a sharp stone in the road of Amaziah's life, a stone upon which Uzziah would one day trip and fall. God does not take a divided heart lightly. In fact, we find this clarion call trumpeted throughout the Old Testament and echoed in the New Testament:

> "You shall love the Lord your God with all your heart and with all your soul and with all your might." (Deut. 6:5)

The most sought-after territory on earth is not the oil fields of Saudi Arabia or the diamond mines of South Africa. It's your heart! Every war that has ever been waged pales in comparison to the white-hot battle being waged for your heart. To save you from your sin, God sacrificed His only Son. If you love God, but not with your whole heart . . . if you serve God, but not with your whole heart . . . then a portion of your heart is unclaimed territory. If you surrender even the smallest piece of your heart to Satan, he may gain a foothold that will allow him to undermine your loyalty to the Lord.

Following in his father's footsteps, Uzziah got off to a great start on his "yellow-brick road" to prosperity.

He did right in the sight of the Lord according to all that his father Amaziah had done. He continued to seek God in the days of Zechariah, who had understanding through the vision of God; and as long as he sought the Lord, God prospered him. (2 Chron. 26:4–5)

Uzziah as a Statesman

The bricks on the road to Uzziah's prosperity gleamed with the golden touch of God's blessing:

> Now he went out and warred against the Philistines, and broke down the wall of Gath and the wall of Jabneh and the wall of Ashdod; and he built cities in the area of Ashdod and among the Philistines. God helped him against the Philistines, and against the Arabians who lived in Gur-baal, and the Meunites. The Ammonites also gave tribute to Uzziah, and his fame extended to the border of Egypt, for he became very strong. Moreover, Uzziah built towers in Jerusalem at the Corner Gate and at the Valley Gate and at the corner buttress and fortified them. He built towers in the wilderness and hewed many cisterns, for he had much livestock, both in the lowland and in the plain. He also had plowmen and vinedressers in the hill country and the fertile fields, for he loved the soil. Moreover, Uzziah had an army ready for battle, which entered combat by divisions according to the number of their muster, prepared by Jeiel the scribe and Maaseiah the official, under the direction of Hananiah, one of the king's officers. The total number of the heads of the households, of valiant warriors, was 2,600. Under their direction was an elite army of 307,500, who could wage war with great power, to help the king against the enemy. Moreover, Uzziah prepared for all the army shields, spears, helmets, body armor, bows and sling stones. In Jerusalem he made engines of war invented by skillful men to be on the towers and on the corners for the purpose of shooting arrows and great stones. Hence his fame spread afar, for he was marvelously helped until he was strong. (vv. 6–15)

Politically, Uzziah's leadership resulted in triumph over his enemies (vv. 6–8) and great accomplishments in his kingdom (vv. 9–10).
Militarily, he was organized, prepared (vv. 11–14), and inventive
(v. 15). *Personally*, "his fame extended to the border of Egypt, for he
became very strong" (v. 8, see also v. 15).

Uzziah as a Rebel

Tragically, however, Uzziah started to believe his own press clip-
pings. As he skipped footloose through the poppy fields of his own
pride, Uzziah began to forget that it was God who had helped him
prosper.

> But when he became strong, his heart was so proud
> that he acted corruptly, and he was unfaithful to the
> Lord his God, for he entered the temple of the Lord
> to burn incense on the altar of incense. Then Azariah
> the priest entered after him and with him eighty
> priests of the Lord, valiant men. They opposed Uzziah
> the king and said to him, "It is not for you, Uzziah,
> to burn incense to the Lord, but for the priests, the
> sons of Aaron who are consecrated to burn incense.
> Get out of the sanctuary, for you have been unfaith-
> ful and will have no honor from the Lord God."
> (vv. 16–18)

In his book *Mere Christianity*, C. S. Lewis discusses man's greatest sin—pride.

> The essential vice, the utmost evil, is Pride. Unchas-
> tity, anger, greed, drunkenness, and all that, are mere
> fleabites in comparison: it was through Pride that the
> devil became the devil: Pride leads to every other vice:
> it is the complete anti-God state of mind.
> . . . As long as you are proud you cannot know God.
> A proud man is always looking down on things and
> people: and, of course, as long as you are looking
> down, you cannot see something that is above you.[2]

2. C. S. Lewis, as quoted in *A Mind Awake: An Anthology of C. S. Lewis*, ed. Clyde S. Kilby
(New York, N.Y.: Harcourt, Brace and World, 1969), p. 115.

Uzziah as a Leper

Preening over his strength, Uzziah believed himself to be bigger than life, thus totally crowding God out of the scene.

> But Uzziah, with a censer in his hand for burning incense, was enraged; and while he was enraged with the priests, the leprosy broke out on his forehead before the priests in the house of the Lord, beside the altar of incense. Azariah the chief priest and all the priests looked at him, and behold, he was leprous on his forehead; and they hurried him out of there, and he himself also hastened to get out because the Lord had smitten him. King Uzziah was a leper to the day of his death; and he lived in a separate house, being a leper, for he was cut off from the house of the Lord. And Jotham his son was over the king's house judging the people of the land.
>
> Now the rest of the acts of Uzziah, first to last, the prophet Isaiah, the son of Amoz, has written. So Uzziah slept with his fathers, and they buried him with his fathers in the field of the grave which belonged to the kings, for they said, "He is a leper." And Jotham his son became king in his place. (2 Chron. 26:19–23)

We find the words "He is a leper" chiseled into the historical granite of Scripture—a tragic epitaph to one whose fame once reached the borders of the mighty Egyptian empire.

A Closing Epitaph

Nathaniel Hawthorne was correct when he said: "A grave, wherever it is found, preaches a short and pithy sermon to the soul."[3] If you were to die today, what words do you think would be used to describe you and your life? If you had the choice, what would you *want* God and others to say about you?

---

3. Nathaniel Hawthorne, as quoted in *1,001 Sermon Illustrations and Quotations*, comp. Geikie, Cowper, and others (Grand Rapids, Mich.: Baker Book House, 1954), p. 54.

Living Insights

Prosperity followed Uzziah as long as he sought the Lord (2 Chron. 26:5). Look up each of the following verses from the Book of Psalms. What do they tell us about seeking the Lord?

Psalm 9:9–10 _____

_____

Psalm 22:26 _____

_____

Psalm 24:1–6 _____

_____

Psalm 34:9–10 _____

_____

Psalm 70:4 _____

_____

Psalm 105:3–4 _____

_____

Although we may recognize God as our refuge, our strength, and our source of blessing, once prosperity comes, it's easy to focus on the blessings in the foreground rather than on His hand in the background. When that happens, the only hand we tend to see in the picture is our own, thus paving the way for an unhealthy, prideful ego trip.

God's warning to the Israelites before they entered into the blessings of the Promised Land serves to correct our vision:

> "Beware that you do not forget the Lord your God . . . otherwise, when you have eaten and are satisfied . . . and when your herds and your flocks multiply, and your silver and gold multiply, and all that you have multiplies, then your heart will become

proud and you will forget the Lord your God who brought you out from the land of Egypt, out of the house of slavery. He led you through the great and terrible wilderness, with its fiery serpents and scorpions and thirsty ground where there was no water; He brought water for you out of the rock of flint. In the wilderness He fed you manna which your fathers did not know, that He might humble you and that He might test you, to do good for you in the end. Otherwise, you may say in your heart, 'My power and the strength of my hand made me this wealth.' But you shall remember the Lord your God, for it is He who is giving you power to make wealth." (Deut. 8:11–18)

Take a few moments to inventory your blessings. Perhaps your spouse, children, family, health, friends, home, job, and material possessions come to mind. (If you're facing extremely tough circumstances these days, this exercise may be a real challenge, but keep thinking!) Jot down several specific blessings for which you are thankful.

_____

_____

_____

_____

_____

_____

_____

_____

_____

Whose hand do you see providing these marvelous blessings in your life? If you have to squint to see God's hand, maybe it's time to readjust your focus. Remember: "*In Him* we live and move and exist" (Acts 17:28, emphasis added). Conversely, *without Him,* we can do nothing. Therefore, to Him, and Him alone, we should gratefully offer our honor, worship, and praise.

Questions for Group Discussion

1. In what ways did Uzziah begin to stray from God's commands? What was the eventual result?

2. How did Uzziah's pride become his downfall?

3. In what ways do you struggle with pride in your own life? How do you overcome the temptation to be prideful?

4. When you come to the end of your life, how do you want to be characterized? What goals would you like to have accomplished?

5. If you could choose the epitaph to be engraved on your tombstone, what would you want it to say?

Chapter 9

FROM CAPTIVE TO QUEEN: AN ADOPTION STORY

Romans 8; Galatians 4; Esther

Most of us don't have to look abortion directly in the eyes. We may read about it, shudder at the thought of it, even campaign against it. But we never really get close enough to see its face. Only the few who enclose themselves within the cold, clean walls to watch or participate in the act . . . only they understand what really happens.

While abortion is a sad reality, we can rejoice that we have an alternative—the light and warmth of adoption. It extends a hand of healing, restoration, and hope to all involved.

When an adoptive couple finally holds their precious child in their arms, they are saved from the anguish of infertility, the anxiety of waiting to have a family, or other tragic circumstances they may have faced. The living, breathing bundle of joy helps to soothe their pain and lessen their sense of loss. And the child is rescued, too—from being unwanted, from being raised by unwilling or unprepared parents, maybe even from having his or her precious life snuffed out. Adoption is God's candle of hope in the dark night of infertility and abortion.

In this lesson, we'll see how God used Esther's adoption to raise her status from an orphaned captive to a beloved queen. Likewise, we'll discover that we've been transformed from struggling sinners to joint heirs with the King of Kings.

The Theology of Adoption

Romans 8 is the magnum opus of Paul's theological statement about life with God. Specifically, Paul talks about some of the benefits of being connected with God's family (vv. 1–15). First, we are protected *forever* from God's condemnation (v. 1). Second, we are set free from the oppressive bondage of sin and death (v. 2). Third, we receive the power of the Holy Spirit, which enables us to resist temptation and walk "according to the Spirit" (v. 4). Fourth, we gain the mind of the Spirit, which is "life and peace" (v. 6). Fifth, we have the righteousness of God (v. 10). Sixth, we have assurance that we will be resurrected from the dead (v. 13). What wonderful blessings await those who've been adopted into God's family!

Galatians 4 underscores these rich truths about adoption.

> God sent forth His Son, born of a woman, born under the Law, so that He might redeem those who were under the Law, that we might receive the adoption as sons. (Gal. 4:4–5)

The term *adoption* is resplendent with meaning. It comes from a combination of two Greek words: *huios*, meaning "son," and *tithemi*, which means "to sit, to place, to put." The result is the term *huiothesia*, which means "the placement of a son."(For more references to adoption, see Romans 9:4 and Ephesians 1:5.) Interestingly, in ancient biblical culture, a natural-born son could be disowned, but an adopted son could not. He remained a part of his father's family for life. Because we have been adopted as sons and heirs through Jesus (Gal. 4:7), we're part of His family for all eternity and are entitled to a wealth of privileges and responsibilities.

The Greek word for *redemption* in Galatians 4:5 above refers to "the price of redeeming something that is in pawn; money paid to ransom prisoners of war; money paid to buy a slave's freedom." In other words, God reached into the slave market of sin, broke our fetters, and redeemed us when we made the choice to come to Him by faith. We are no longer slaves, but heirs. Titus 2:13–14 lists the price of our redemption: "our great God and Savior, Christ Jesus, who *gave Himself* for us" (emphasis added).

Strangely, many of us who have accepted God's free gift of salvation are still trying to find a way to pay Him back. We come to God with one hand extended and the other groping around in our pockets for loose change. It's our instinct to want to pay our debts—to even things up. We tend to think that the more church committees we join, small groups we lead, and Third World children we sponsor, the more worthy we'll be of God's gift of eternal life.

The gift of salvation did come at a great price—God's only begotten Son. But He offers it to us free of charge, without strings or buy-now, pay-later conditions. It's been *completely* paid for by Jesus Christ.

A Biography of Adoption

In the form of a biography, the Book of Esther illustrates the theological truth of adoption. Esther, a young Jewish orphan, was mercifully adopted by her cousin Mordecai (Est. 2:5–7). This drama stars three more characters: Ahasuerus, king of Persia, also known as Xerxes; Vashti, the king's beautiful wife; and Haman, the haughty villain.

Of the sixty-six books in the Bible, Esther is the only one that doesn't mention the name of God. But, although His name is absent, His providential fingerprints can be found throughout. Replete with action and intrigue, this ancient story of adoption still speaks to us about God's sovereign plan and protection of His people.

A Feast Marked by Punishment

As the story goes, King Ahasuerus threw a big bash for the entire populace of Susa, the capital city of the Persian Empire (1:5). During the seven days of this revelry, "the royal wine was plentiful according to the king's bounty" (v. 7). On the seventh day, when "the king was merry with wine," he decided to send for Queen Vashti to come in and parade her beauty in front of his guests (vv. 10–11).

But Vashti said no, which, in her day, was not a popular thing to do. Many modern women would have applauded Vashti's liberated conduct and views, but not King Ahasuerus. His wrath burned so hotly within him that he sought counsel on what disciplinary measures he should take with Vashti (vv. 12–15). Concerned that the queen's rebellion would cause other married women in the Persian kingdom to disobey their husbands, the king was advised to ban her from his presence and replace her with a "more worthy" woman (v. 19).

An Ancient Beauty Contest

To find Vashti's replacement, the king staged a beauty pageant. The entire kingdom was scoured so he could choose the most beautiful young virgin. Mordecai entered Esther in the contest, advising her not to reveal her Jewish background. And, as the finger of God began to move through the streets of Susa, it landed sovereignly on Esther.

> The king loved Esther more than all the women,
> and she found favor and kindness with him more than
> all the virgins, so that he set the royal crown on her
> head and made her queen instead of Vashti. (2:17)

A Crucial Subplot

After this climactic scene, the camera seems to wander to an extraneous subplot. Mordecai learns of a scheme to assassinate the king and reports it to Esther, who then informs the king "in Mordecai's name" (v. 22). After a thorough investigation, Mordecai's information is verified, the two conspirators are hanged, and it is "written in the Book of the Chronicles in the king's presence" (v. 23).

Tuck this scene away in your mind until later. After seeing God's sovereign plan, we will understand its significance.

A Promotion and a Plot

Meanwhile, Haman is promoted to become the king's right-hand man, and the king commands everyone to pay homage to Haman. But Mordecai, aware of Haman's greed and conceit, "neither bowed down nor paid homage" (3:2). And he was not about to be excused for such disobedience.

> When Haman saw that Mordecai neither bowed down nor paid homage to him, Haman was filled with rage. But he disdained to lay hands on Mordecai alone, for they had told him who the people of Mordecai were; therefore Haman sought to destroy all the Jews, the people of Mordecai, who were throughout the whole kingdom of Ahasuerus. (vv. 5–6)

An ancient Holocaust took shape in the mind of this Old Testament Hitler, and then Haman unveiled his evil plot to the king.

> Then Haman said to King Ahasuerus, "There is a certain people scattered and dispersed among the peoples in all the provinces of your kingdom; their laws are different from those of all other people and they do not observe the king's laws, so it is not in the king's interest to let them remain. If it is pleasing to the king, let it be decreed that they be destroyed, and I will pay ten thousand talents of silver into the hands of those who carry on the king's business, to put into the king's treasuries." (vv. 8–9)

The king's response undoubtedly made Haman grin:

> Then the king took his signet ring from his hand and gave it to Haman . . . , the enemy of the Jews. The king said to Haman, "The silver is yours, and the people also, to do with them as you please." (vv. 10–11)

A Creative Plan

After discovering Haman's plot, Mordecai and all the people mourned (4:1–3). When Esther heard of the plot, she inquired about the details, but stopped short of offering any real help (vv. 4–12).

Mordecai then sent this convicting word by way of a messenger:

> "Do not imagine that you in the king's palace can escape any more than all the Jews. For if you remain silent at this time, relief and deliverance will arise for the Jews from another place and you and your father's house will perish. And who knows whether you have not attained royalty for such a time as this?" (4:13–14)

Talk about great rhetoric! It's as if Mordecai is saying, "This is your meeting with destiny, Esther. This is why God had me take you as a little girl and raise you according to His commands. This is God's work. Don't be silent. Speak up!" And Esther gave this reply to Mordecai:

> "Go, assemble all the Jews who are found in Susa, and fast for me; do not eat or drink for three days, night or day. I and my maidens also will fast in the same way. And thus I will go in to the king, which is not according to the law; and if I perish, I perish." (v. 16)

Risking her life, Esther appeared before the king without a summons. He openly welcomed her into his presence and beckoned her to make her request. She diverted his attention momentarily, inviting him and Haman to a banquet she had prepared. While dining together, she invited them to a banquet on the next day, promising to reveal her request (5:1–8).

Pleased with being considered part of the royalty, his head swelling with pride, Haman left the feast. However, his good feelings were squelched at the sight of Mordecai, who still refused to bow down to him. Enraged, Haman plotted to have Mordecai hanged the next morning (5:9–14).

A Look Within

Before we get swept away by the unfolding drama of the story, let's take a moment to get a close-up of Esther. If there were a scale that measured faith against works, Esther would weigh in evenly. Note her well-balanced response to Mordecai's plea. Notice how she asks the Jews to fast with her for three days, to display externally the seriousness of their prayers to God. Also consider her words, "If I perish, I perish" (4:16), which demonstrate her firm confidence in God's plan. She exhibited a graceful, winning combination of faith and follow-through.

The same thing should be true of our Christian lives today. God's gift of salvation is free—received by faith alone. But our works are its vital signs, proof that our faith is alive and active (see James 2:17–18). Take a look at the New Testament scale in perfect balance:

> For by grace you have been saved through faith; and that not of yourselves, *it is the gift of God; not as a result of works,* so that no one may boast. For we are His workmanship, created in Christ Jesus for good works, which God prepared beforehand so that we would walk in them. (Eph. 2:8–10, emphasis added)

Is the faith pan of your spiritual scale scraping the tabletop, while the works pan hangs elevated and empty? Or is your scale tipped toward the works tray, leaving the faith tray sorely wanting?

A Reading of Remembrance and Overdue Honor

That night, while the gallows was being built, King Ahasuerus couldn't sleep, "so he gave an order to bring the book of records, the chronicles, and they were read before the king" (Est. 6:1). Reminded that Mordecai had tipped him off about the conspiracy, King Ahasuerus decided to honor him. So the king sent for Haman and asked, "What is to be done for the man whom the king desires to honor?" (v. 6). Certain that the king wants to honor him, Haman answered:[1]

> "For the man whom the king desires to honor, let them bring a royal robe which the king has worn, and the horse on which the king has ridden, and on whose head a royal crown has been placed; and let the robe and the horse be handed over to one of the king's most noble princes and let them array the man whom the king desires to honor and lead him on horseback through the city square, and proclaim before him, 'Thus it shall be done to the man whom the king desires to honor.'" (vv. 7–9)

---

1. Theologian Merrill Unger comments on Haman's pride: "What an illustration of the truth that 'pride goeth before destruction, and a haughty spirit before a fall' (Prov. 16:18; [compare] 18:12). The honors Haman's pride would bestow upon himself were to be bestowed upon his enemy, Mordecai, the Jew, hatred for whom had deprived him of all sense and reason, and like all his ilk, made him a colossal megalomaniac." Merrill F. Unger, *Unger's Commentary on the Old Testament* (Chicago, Ill.: Moody Press, 1981), vol. 1, p. 665.

The king took Haman's advice. But to Haman's shame, *he* had to honor *Mordecai*. What dramatic irony! After carrying out the king's wishes, Haman "hurried home, mourning, with his head covered" (Est. 6:12).

Exposure and Justice

That evening, at Esther's banquet, the king again asks Esther to reveal her request:

> Then Queen Esther replied, "If I have found favor in your sight, O king, and if it please the king, let my life be given me as my petition, and my people as my request; for we have been sold, I and my people, to be destroyed, to be killed and to be annihilated. Now if we had only been sold as slaves, men and women, I would have remained silent, for the trouble would not be commensurate with the annoyance to the king." (7:3–4)

The king asks Esther, "Who is he, and where is he, who would presume to do thus?" (v. 5). Esther responds, "A foe and an enemy is this wicked Haman!" (v. 6). The king, outraged, had Haman hung on the very gallows he had built to execute Mordecai. Haman's plot to destroy the Jews was foiled because of the courage of Esther, an adopted woman who risked her life to save her people. The book closes with the Feast of Purim (meaning "Peace"), which is still celebrated by Jews today in Esther's honor (8:1–10:3).

The Practicality of Adoption

Esther's story illustrates the beauty of adoption. Remembering these three truths will help us grasp the unique significance of it.

First: *The adoption process best models the way people enter God's family.* Families with adopted children are living illustrations of salvation. Like adoptive parents, who reach into humanity and choose a child—and not on the child's merit—God has mercifully reached out and said, "You're unique, and you're Mine."

Second: *Adopted children often become God's special instruments.* As He did with Esther, God sometimes chooses adopted children to fulfill His special purposes. Their destinies have been changed! Many have been preserved, rescued from dire circumstances in order that they may fulfill God's purposes in the light of His love.

Third: *People who are touched by the adopted realize how profound God's plan is.* If you've brushed lives with adopted children or adults, you have been given a glimpse into the graciousness of God's redemptive design.

Like an adopted child who was not aborted but given a new lease on life, our destinies were altered when we became part of God's family. The individual pearls of our lives have been threaded together to form a beautiful necklace of purpose and meaning. We have been saved from death and have been chosen instead to live abundantly in Jesus Christ.

Living Insights

People have many different thoughts and feelings about adoption. Are you adopted, or do you know of a friend, family member, or coworker who is adopted? How would you describe your (or this person's) experience?

_____

_____

_____

_____

What are the benefits of choosing to offer a child up for adoption rather than choosing abortion?

_____

_____

_____

_____

What are the similarities between being a part of a birth family and being adopted?

_____

_____

_____

_____

What are the differences?

_____

_____

_____

_____

What advantages do adopted people enjoy?

_____

_____

_____

_____

What disadvantages tend to hinder them?

_____

_____

_____

_____

Do you think that society treats adopted children differently? Why or why not?

_____

_____

_____

_____

What have you learned about spiritual adoption that can help you understand and appreciate adoption in the physical realm?

_____

_____

_____

_____

Questions for Group Discussion

1. How was Esther's "adopted" status a hardship for her? In what ways was it a blessing?

2. Describe Mordecai and his role in Esther's life. How did he help her to become a principal player in this drama?

3. In what ways did God uniquely prepare Esther to address the king and save her people from annihilation?

4. What lessons can we glean from seeing the results of Haman's haughtiness and pride?

5. What hope does this story offer to adopted children and their parents?

Chapter 10

MR. JONES, MEET
MR. JONAH

Jonah

Written in 1851 by Herman Melville, the book *Moby-Dick*
breached the sea of world literature to surface as an international classic. In chapter 9, one of Melville's characters, Father
Mapple, begins a sermon on the Book of Jonah:

> "Shipmates, this book, containing only four chapters—
> four yarns—is one of the smallest strands in the mighty
> cable of the Scriptures. Yet what depths of the soul
> does Jonah's deep sea-line sound! What a pregnant
> lesson to us is this prophet! What a noble thing is
> that canticle in the fish's belly! How billow-like and
> boisterously grand! We feel the floods surging over us;
> we sound with him to the kelpy bottom of the waters;
> seaweed and all the slime of the sea is about us! But
> *what* is this lesson that the book of Jonah teaches?"[1]

As we set sail on our voyage into Jonah, we are captivated by
the story's high-seas drama. At the same time, our lives are plumbed
by its emotion and anchored by its application. A whale may come
to mind when we consider the story of Jonah. However, like *Moby-
Dick*, Jonah is not simply a story about a whale but a drama involv-
ing a man, nature, and God. Before we loosen our moorings to embark
onto the open seas, let's load a few pieces of introductory cargo.

Was Jonah Fictional or Factual?

The first crate we must take aboard is this weighty issue: Did a
man by the name of Jonah actually live? Second Kings 14:23–25
answers this question, recording Jonah's name as a historical fact:

> In the fifteenth year of Amaziah the son of Joash
> king of Judah, Jeroboam the son of Joash king of Israel

---

1. Herman Melville, *Moby-Dick; or, The Whale*, in vol. 48 of *Great Books of the Western World*,
ed. Robert Maynard Hutchins (Chicago, Ill.: Encyclopaedia Britannica, 1971), p. 31.

became king in Samaria, and reigned forty-one years. He did evil in the sight of the Lord; he did not depart from all the sins of Jeroboam the son of Nebat, which he made Israel sin. He restored the border of Israel from the entrance of Hamath as far as the Sea of the Arabah, according to the word of the Lord, the God of Israel, which He spoke through His servant Jonah the son of Amittai, the prophet, who was of Gath-hepher.

We know that Jeroboam was a real king, that Hamath and the Sea of the Arabah were real places, and that Israel was a real nation. Therefore, it is logical to assume that Jonah, too, was a real person. Critics, however, might respond by saying that this reference concerned another prophet named Jonah, not the one depicted in the Book of Jonah. But, if we compare 2 Kings 14:25 with Jonah 1:1–2, the descriptions appear to be identical. Both men are prophets, both are named Jonah, and both are referred to as the "son of Amittai."

Another passage that affirms the existence of Jonah is Matthew 12:38–41, where Jesus Himself asserts that Jonah was a living prophet:

> Then some of the scribes and Pharisees said to Him, "Teacher, we want to see a sign from You." But He answered and said to them, "An evil and adulterous generation craves for a sign; and yet no sign will be given to it but the sign of Jonah the prophet; for just as Jonah was three days and three nights in the belly of the sea monster, so will the Son of Man be three days and three nights in the heart of the earth. The men of Nineveh will stand up with this generation at the judgment, and will condemn it because they repented at the preaching of Jonah; and behold, something greater than Jonah is here."

Here, the Lord connects a man named Jonah to a real city, Nineveh, as well as to an actual event, the Resurrection. Had Jonah been a mythological character, it is doubtful Jesus would have linked him, even literarily, to so crucial an event as the Resurrection. Jesus called Jonah a prophet (v. 39), mentioned his days in the large fish's belly (v. 40), and noted his preaching (v. 41).

So both 2 Kings and Christ's testimony affirm the authenticity of Jonah. Consequently, we sail in well-charted seas when we hoist the historical flag over Jonah's name.

How Are We to Understand the Book?

Turning our attention from the person of Jonah to the Book of Jonah is like turning our faces to the biting winds of a severe storm. No book in the Bible has been as badly battered by a sea of criticism as Jonah has. Some people believe the book is a parable—an earthly story with a heavenly meaning—similar to the parable of the prodigal son (Luke 15:11–32). But this view disregards the fact that Christ, in the same book (11:29–30), regards Jonah as a historical person.

Some see the book as an allegory, like John Bunyan's *The Pilgrim's Progress*, where the story's true meaning can only be found by translating its characters and events into the truths they symbolize. Jonah's narrative, however, lacks the obvious allegorical signposts of *The Pilgrim's Progress*, where the protagonist, Christian, encounters characters with names like "Great Despair" and "Mr. Worldly Wiseman" on his journey to the Celestial City. In Jonah, all the signs are posted along real routes traveled by real people on their way to real cities.

The final interpretative option is to accept the book at face value—as a historical narrative. The historical places referred to are Nineveh (1:2), Tarshish, and Joppa (v. 3). The population of Nineveh, approximated by some scholars to be around six hundred thousand (based on 4:11, which indicates that more than 120,000 children lived there), is substantiated by archaeological evidence.[2]

This traditional explanation of Jonah as historical narrative has been questioned in modern times due to the miraculous nature of the book's events. Consequently, if you reject the miraculous from the outset, you have to reject the book's historical character as well. But if you accept the miraculous intervention of God in human events, then accepting the book as a straightforward historical account should pose no problem. Certainly, if you accept the miracle of the fish and loaves, then the miracle of the fish and Jonah shouldn't be too hard to swallow!

To understand the book's message, we need to cast a net that catches the essentials and allows the incidentals to slip away. The message is not just the story of a man swallowed by a fish; it's the account of how God dealt with a reluctant and recalcitrant prophet who stubbornly refused to obey Him in carrying His Word to one of Israel's worst enemies.

A motif emerges in the story of Jonah when we divide the book into four parts. In chapter 1, he's running from God; in chapter 2,

---

2. Charles F. Pfeiffer, ed., *The Biblical World: A Dictionary of Biblical Archaeology* (Grand Rapids, Mich.: Baker Book House, 1966), pp. 415–417.

he's running to God; in chapter 3, he's running with God; in chapter 4, he's running against God.

Why Didn't Jonah Want to Go to Nineveh?

What would cause God's prophet to flee from His presence? Most commentators list three reasons: fear, prejudice, and pride. Some say Jonah feared venturing into enemy territory. This is doubtful. If he didn't fear the storm or being tossed into the sea, then it seems unlikely that Jonah avoided Nineveh because of fear.

Others say that since Jonah was a Jew, he didn't want to lower himself to taking a message from God to the Gentiles. While on the ship, however, he expressed a deep compassion for the welfare of the idol-worshiping sailors, telling them to toss him overboard if they wanted to stop the storm.

Still others say pride kept Jonah from going to Nineveh. If he went around declaring a message of judgment and the people repented, God would show mercy, and Jonah's prophecy would be null and void. As a result, his credentials as a prophet in Jeroboam's court would be greatly devalued, if not bankrupt altogether.

Why didn't Jonah want to go to Nineveh? The answer is found in chapter 4, verse 2. Jonah states that he ran away to Tarshish because he knew God would show the Ninevites mercy if they repented:

> "Therefore in order to forestall this I fled to Tarshish,
> for I knew that You are a gracious and compassionate
> God, slow to anger and abundant in lovingkindness,
> and one who relents concerning calamity."

Their cup of wickedness was full . . . their days were numbered . . . their doom was certain. This was fine with Jonah, as Nineveh was key to the powerful empire of Assyria, Israel's arch-enemy. The Assyrians were a brutal foe with a thirst for blood and a penchant for vengeance. It is no wonder that Jonah wanted them destroyed. He undoubtedly would have shared Nahum's sentiments as the latter foresaw Nineveh's downfall in 612 B.C.:

> Woe to the bloody city, completely full of lies
> and pillage; . . .
> 'Nineveh is devastated! Who will grieve for her?' . . .
> All who hear about you
> Will clap their hands over you,
> For on whom has not your evil passed continually?
> (Nah. 3:1, 7, 19)

Did a Whale Actually Swallow Jonah?

The next bit of introductory baggage deals with the whale in our tale. First, the text says the whale was "appointed" by God (1:17). The Hebrew term for *appointed, manah,* is used in the sense of assigning or ordaining. Second, the Hebrew term *dag gadol* literally means "great fish," not "whale." In the New Testament, this term is translated *ketos,* meaning "sea monster" (see Matt. 12:40). What's in view here may be a whale, a shark, or some type of large fish.

But could an enormous fish really swallow a whole man? Interpreting the "great fish" of Jonah 1:17 to possibly mean a whale, R. K. Harrison notes several reported cases of whales swallowing men alive.

> As regards the credibility of the event described, it has frequently been remarked that the true whale has such a narrow gullet that it could only swallow comparatively small fish, and certainly nothing approaching the size of a man. In this general connection, however, it is important to observe that the Hebrew spoke of a "great fish" (Jon. 1:17), that is to say, some kind of sea denizen, and that the interpretation "whale" is the result of translations into English. Furthermore, while the true whale, whose habitat is the Arctic Ocean rather than the Mediterranean Sea, cannot swallow a man, the sperm whale or *cachalot* most probably can. Despite this constitutional obstacle it was shown as long ago as 1915 that even a true whale could save a man from drowning if he managed to negotiate the air-supply tract of the mammal and reach the great laryngeal pouch. . . . On another occasion a whale-hunter was reportedly swallowed in 1891, but was recovered the following day in unconscious condition from the inside of the mammal. Again, a seaman was said to have been swallowed by a large sperm whale in the vicinity of the Falkland Islands, and after three days was recovered unconscious but alive, though with some damage to his skin.[3]

3. Roland Kenneth Harrison, *Introduction to the Old Testament* (Grand Rapids, Mich.: William B. Eerdmans Publishing Co., 1969), p. 907, as originally quoted from the following sources: G. Macloskie, *Bibliotheca Sacra,* vol. 72 (1915), p. 336f; *Neue Lutheranische Kirchenzeitung* (1895), p. 303; A. J. Wilson, *Princeton Theological Review,* vol. 25 (1927), p. 636.

Whether the great fish was a whale, a whale shark, or some other sea creature, the great miracle of Jonah was not that he was swallowed or that he was kept alive for three days. The miracle was the Ninevites' response to the message Jonah preached. One and all, great and small, they repented and transferred their allegiance to the one "Great King"—the Lord of Hosts.

Living Insights

The greatest miracle in the Book of Jonah is not the incident with the great fish. The greatest miracle is one of the most successful evangelistic crusades in the history of the world. Let's get a little closer to home. How does Jonah's life compare with yours?

As with Jonah, is there something that looms large in your relationship with God—something you know that He wants you to do, but you have been avoiding? What do you hope to gain by running? What are you definitely losing by running from it?

_____

_____

_____

_____

Do you or someone you know struggle with feeling that God has "put you on the shelf" because of past disobedience, and that He can no longer use you in a significant way? Why?

_____

_____

_____

_____

What does Jonah's experience tell us about God's willingness to use us in spite of our failures?

_____

_____

_____

_____

_____

Jonah didn't want God to show mercy to Israel's enemies. Is there a person or people you would rather see experience judgment than repentance? What is God's attitude toward them (See Romans 5:6–10; 1 Timothy 2:4)?

_____

_____

_____

How can you align your heart with God's commands? Read Matthew 5:43–48.

_____

_____

_____

How open are you to sharing the Gospel with others? Are there personal, religious, cultural, or economic roadblocks that cause you to detour around certain people? How can you overcome this attitude and fulfill our Lord's Great Commission (see Matthew 28:16–20)?

_____

_____

_____

As you ponder these questions, ask God to guide you to those who need to hear about Him. As you model a giving heart and a willing attitude, God will use you to do His work.

_____

_____

_____

 *Questions for Group Discussion*

1. What did Jonah's attitude and his desire to run from God's call say about him as an individual?

2. What circumstances did God use to change Jonah's heart?

3. How do you think Jonah's experiences at sea affected him physically, emotionally, and spiritually?

4. Has God ever used an unusual circumstance to bring you back to Him? If so, what was it? How did it change you?

5. How did the Ninevites' response to God's call to repentance differ from Jonah's initial response to God's command? What does this say about them?

6. Have you noticed that so much of what God wants to communicate through His Word is taught through the real-life stories of actual people, like Jonah? Read 2 Corinthians 3:1–3. What are the people around you—your spouse, children, coworkers, and friends—learning about God through your life? What kind of God does your life describe to them?

Chapter 11

THE PRODIGAL PREACHER

Jonah 1–2

The first two chapters of Jonah show how God dealt with the disobedience of one of His messengers. Like an ancient "wanted" poster, these chapters depict Jonah as a fugitive. In a sermon on Jonah in the book *Moby-Dick*, Father Mapple describes this runaway prophet:

> "With this sin of disobedience in him, Jonah still further flouts at God, by seeking to flee from Him. He thinks that a ship made by men will carry him into countries where God does not reign, but only the Captains of this earth. He skulks about the wharves of Joppa, seeks a ship that's bound for Tarshish. . . . Miserable man! Oh! most contemptible and worthy of all scorn; with slouched hat and guilty eye, skulking from his God; prowling among the shipping like a vile burglar hastening to cross the seas. So disordered, self-condemning is his look, that had there been policemen in those days, Jonah, on the mere suspicion of something wrong, had been arrested ere he touched a deck. How plainly he's a fugitive! No baggage, not a hat-box, valise, or carpet-bag—no friends accompany him to the wharf with their adieux."[1]

Such is the sad, shadowy picture of a man going to great lengths to run from God. We'll find, however, that God goes to even greater lengths to get him back.

God's Command

The book begins in a dramatic and arresting way as God breaks the silence of heaven to give Jonah his missionary orders:

> The word of the Lord came to Jonah the son of Amittai saying, "Arise, go to Nineveh the great city

---

1. Herman Melville, *Moby-Dick; or, The Whale*, in vol. 48 of *Great Books of the Western World*, ed. Robert Maynard Hutchins (Chicago, Ill.: Encyclopaedia Britannica, 1971), p. 31.

and cry against it, for their wickedness has come up before Me." (1:1–2)

Traveling and preaching usually posed no problem for prophets. It was their job! But in this case, even the sound of the word *Nineveh* caused Jonah's stomach to churn. Nineveh was a leading city and future capital of the vicious and godless Assyrians, Israel's archenemy. In every city they conquered, the Assyrians built a pyramid of human skulls. That was the brutal "business card" they left behind. No wonder Jonah responded as he did!

Jonah's Disobedience

From Jonah's perspective, God had finally gone too far. This reluctant prophet felt that by calling him to take His message to Nineveh, the Lord was asking way too much. So instead of arising, going, and crying out, Jonah arose, fled, and shipped out. In disobedience, he headed to Tarshish, over two thousand miles away from Nineveh and the westernmost point on any trade route:

> But Jonah rose up to flee to Tarshish from the presence of the Lord. So he went down to Joppa, found a ship which was going to Tarshish, paid the fare and went down into it to go with them to Tarshish from the presence of the Lord. (v. 3)

Have you ever tried to flee from the presence of God when you felt that He was asking too much of you? Have you ever felt frustrated when He asked you to get outside your comfort zone or think outside the box? If so, you've got company. But fleeing from the Lord is like trying to draw a round square. It's a logical impossibility. God is omnipresent—everywhere—and you can't escape from Someone who is everywhere. The Psalmist supports this truth in one of the best-loved passages of the Bible:

> Where can I go from Your Spirit?
> Or where can I flee from Your presence?
> If I ascend to heaven, You are there;
> If I make my bed in Sheol, behold, You are there.
> If I take the wings of the dawn,
> If I dwell in the remotest part of the sea,
> Even there Your hand will lead me,
> And Your right hand will lay hold of me.
> If I say, "Surely the darkness will overwhelm me,

And the light around me will be night,"
Even the darkness is not dark to You,
And the night is as bright as the day.
Darkness and light are alike to You. (Ps. 139:7–12)

Whether you're deep in a cave, high on the cliffs of a mountain, or on a ship in the middle of the ocean, God is there. When you're grieving, depressed, ill, or hurting, He is there. When you've lost your moorings and feel like you're drifting in a sea of sin and immorality, He is there. He hears your cries for help, and when you call to Him, He will rescue you—not just from your circumstances, but from yourself.

God's Response to Jonah's Disobedience

God's plan to deliver Nineveh (see 2 Peter 3:9) was not thwarted by this stubborn, strong-willed prophet, regardless of his credentials. God harnessed the wild winds of nature to hunt down this fugitive:

> The Lord hurled a great wind on the sea and there
> was a great storm on the sea so that the ship was about
> to break up. (Jonah 1:4)

When we're disobedient to God, our actions often have a negative effect, bringing a storm into our lives that can shipwreck the lives of those around us. However, the storm God sends is not meant to sweep us out to sea, but to bring us home. Notice how God's hunt for the prodigal prophet is tenaciously active: "The Lord *hurled* a great wind" (emphasis added). Apparently, this storm was so great that even the seasoned sailors on board feared for their lives and resorted to drastic measures:

> Then the sailors became afraid and every man cried
> to his god, and they threw the cargo which was in
> the ship into the sea to lighten it for them. But Jonah
> had gone below into the hold of the ship, lain down
> and fallen sound asleep. (v. 5)

It's been said, "There are no atheists at sea." These sailors give evidence of that! Notice, however, where Jonah is—safe below deck, sound asleep. But the frenzied captain soon wakes him:

> So the captain approached him and said, "How is it
> that you are sleeping? Get up, call on your god. Per-
> haps your god will be concerned about us so that we
> will not perish."

> Each man said to his mate, "Come, let us cast lots
> so we may learn on whose account this calamity has
> struck us." So they cast lots and the lot fell on Jonah.
> Then they said to him, "Tell us, now! On whose
> account has this calamity struck us? What is your
> occupation? And where do you come from? What is
> your country? From what people are you?" (vv. 6–8)

Once the finger of accusation is pointed at Jonah, the prophet
reveals his identity and testifies.

> He said to them, "I am a Hebrew, and I fear the Lord
> God of heaven who made the sea and the dry land."
> (v. 9)

Immediately, the sailors put this missing piece of information into
the puzzle of the sudden storm.

> Then the men became extremely frightened and
> they said to him, "How could you do this?" For the
> men knew that he was fleeing from the presence of
> the Lord, because he had told them. (v. 10)

Desperately, the sailors plead with Jonah for a way to calm the storm:

> So they said to him, "What should we do to you that
> the sea may become calm for us?"—for the sea was
> becoming increasingly stormy. He said to them, "Pick
> me up and throw me into the sea. Then the sea will
> become calm for you, for I know that on account of
> me this great storm has come upon you." However,
> the men rowed desperately to return to land but they
> could not, for the sea was becoming even stormier
> against them. (vv. 11–13)

Hesitant to take a man's life, the sailors try to ride out the storm.
Finally, exhausting their human effort at the oars, the unbelieving
sailors turn to God.

> Then they called on the Lord and said, "We earnestly
> pray, O Lord, do not let us perish on account of this
> man's life and do not put innocent blood on us; for
> You, O Lord, have done as You have pleased."
> So they picked up Jonah, threw him into the sea,
> and the sea stopped its raging. (vv. 14–15)

The sudden, miraculous calming of the sea created an equally miraculous change in the lives of the sailors:

> Then the men feared the Lord greatly, and they offered
> a sacrifice to the Lord and made vows. (v. 16)

God's Salvation

God's salvation extends not only to the pagans spiritually, but goes even further to save the prophet physically. God does not abandon Jonah, regardless of his disobedience, but, in an act of grace, snatches him safely away.

> And the Lord appointed a great fish to swallow
> Jonah, and Jonah was in the stomach of the fish three
> days and three nights. (v. 17)

The brief description of Jonah's ordeal "in the stomach of the fish three days and three nights" seems crisp and clean. But use your imagination to recreate the scene. It's pitch black. You inhale the most powerful stench you've ever smelled. Gastric juices wash over you, burning your skin, eyes, throat, and nostrils. Oxygen is scarce. Each frantic gulp of air is saturated with salt water. Everything you touch has the slimy feel of the mucous membrane that lines the creature's stomach. You feel claustrophobic. With every turn and dive of the great fish, you slip and slide in a cesspool of digestive fluid. There are no footholds, and no blankets to keep you warm.

For three days and three nights Jonah endures this harsh womb of God's grace. His grace sometimes comes to us in ways we would never expect. Does God have you in the stomach of some dark, slippery, distasteful circumstances? If so, prayer is a lamp by which you can see through the darkness and to the Savior's grace.

Jonah's Prayer

From the murky depths of despair, Jonah calls out to God for deliverance.

> Then Jonah prayed to the Lord his God from the
> stomach of the fish, and he said,
> "I called out of my distress to the Lord,
> And He answered me.
> I cried for help from the depth of Sheol;
> You heard my voice.

For You had cast me into the deep,
Into the heart of the seas,
And the current engulfed me.
All Your breakers and billows passed over me.
So I said, 'I have been expelled from Your sight.
Nevertheless I will look again toward Your holy
    temple.'
Water encompassed me to the point of death.
The great deep engulfed me,
Weeds were wrapped around my head.
I descended to the roots of the mountains.
The earth with its bars was around me forever,
But You have brought up my life from the pit,
    O Lord my God.
While I was fainting away,
I remembered the Lord,
And my prayer came to You,
Into Your holy temple.
Those who regard vain idols
Forsake their faithfulness,
But I will sacrifice to You
With the voice of thanksgiving.
That which I have vowed I will pay.
Salvation is from the Lord."
Then the Lord commanded the fish, and it
    vomited Jonah up onto the dry land. (2:1–10)

Jonah cries out in verse 3: "For You had cast me into the deep." But wasn't it the sailors who threw him overboard? Yes, but Jonah sees that, ultimately, God is behind his circumstances. That's looking at life from God's point of view. That's insightful wisdom. Prayer brings perspective in the face of trials. Regarding endurance in the face of trials, James writes: "But if any of you lacks wisdom, let him ask of God, who gives to all generously and without reproach, and it will be given to him" (1:5).

Sometimes it's difficult to see God's hand stirring the storm. There are times when we are thrown overboard and fail to recognize that He is doing the tossing. There are times, too, when we are swallowed by monstrous circumstances and held captive (Jonah 2:6), and we fail to understand that our situation was "appointed" by God. Prayer can give us the perspective we need in order to see God at work in our lives.

If the prayer in Jonah 2 teaches us anything, it instructs us that we can pray anytime, anywhere, and have confidence that no matter how suffocating and slimy our circumstances, our prayers will reach the Lord God of heaven in His holy temple (v. 7).

Living Insights

In this study, we call Jonah "The Prodigal Preacher." In what ways was he a prodigal?

_____

_____

_____

_____

Read the parable of the prodigal son in Luke 15:11–32. What stands out to you from this passage?

_____

_____

_____

_____

How are Jonah and the prodigal son similar?

_____

_____

_____

_____

How are they different?

_____

_____

_____

_____

What do we learn about our Father from both of these Scripture passages?

_____

_____

_____

_____

_____

 Questions for Group Discussion

1. Do you have anything in common with Jonah, the reluctant prophet? If so, what?

2. Spiritually, how would you describe Jonah as a person?

3. What positive character qualities did Jonah possess? Which of his characteristics weren't so positive?

4. If you were to receive a message similar to the one Jonah received, how do you think you would respond? Why?

5. How does the message of the Book of Jonah apply to our calling to share the Gospel with others?

Chapter 12

REVIVAL!
IN SPITE OF THE EVANGELIST

Jonah 3–4

The greatest revival in the history of the world took place in an unlikely spot. John Knox didn't ignite it in Scotland. John Wesley didn't lead it in England. Calvin, Luther, Zwingli, and Savonarola didn't spearhead it in Europe. Neither Jonathan Edwards, nor D. L. Moody, nor Billy Sunday, nor Billy Graham sparked it in the United States.

Stumped? The greatest revival occurred 150 miles northwest of Baghdad, near the modern city of Mosul. In the vicinity of Mosul is a massive mound of earth. Beneath that mound, we are told, is the ancient tomb of the evangelist responsible for this great revival—the prophet Jonah. The mound is named *Nebi Yunus,* Hebrew for "Prophet Jonah."[1]

When we think of Jonah, we think of resistance, rebellion, and retreat. But what should stand out in our thinking is revival, for through this prophet's preaching, the entire city of Nineveh experienced a dramatic conversion to faith in God.

So far, we have seen Jonah running from God in chapter 1 and to God in chapter 2. As our study opens in chapter 3, we see him running with God in obedience.

Jonah's Revival

After walking out on the job, Jonah returns to God with a repentant heart and is given a second chance. He embarks on the single greatest missionary effort of all time.

Physically, the journey was difficult. Jonah's trek from the eastern shore of the Mediterranean to Nineveh spanned approximately five hundred miles. Politically, he was traveling in enemy territory, which made the journey worse. Spiritually, the assignment was undoubtedly hard for Jonah too, as he was given no latitude with regard to his

---

1. Merrill F. Unger, *Archaeology and the Old Testament* (Grand Rapids, Mich.: Zondervan Publishing House, 1970), p. 263.

message. God instructed him: "Proclaim to it the proclamation which I am going to tell you" (v. 2).

In verse 3, Nineveh is described as "an exceedingly great city, a three days' walk." As Californians designate Los Angeles to incorporate many smaller cities and suburbs, so the Hebrews designated several cities within the Nineveh metropolis:

> From that land he went forth into Assyria, and built Nineveh and Rehoboth-Ir and Calah, and Resen between Nineveh and Calah; that is the great city. (Gen. 10:11–12)

Therefore, a three days' walk through the city would be entirely reasonable. During the first monotonous day of his walk, Jonah trudges the streets of this foreign metropolis—one small man calling out like a town crier against this sprawling Sodom of a city. Like a broken record, he parrots the same song: "Yet forty days and Nineveh will be overthrown! Yet forty days and Nineveh will be overthrown! Yet forty days and Nineveh will be overthrown" (see Jonah 3:4)!

Before we see the results of Jonah's repetitive cry, let's backtrack a little and pay special attention to one particular statement: "Now the word of the Lord came to Jonah *the second time*" (Jonah 3:1, emphasis added). This brief phrase reveals a great deal about God's character. He doesn't turn a deaf ear or a cold shoulder to the repentant, no matter how blatant the rebellion may be or which borders the runaway may cross. Like the father in the story of the prodigal son, God waits with open arms. He has the fatted calf, robe, and ring waiting. He wants to give us a second chance to serve Him with a grateful heart and a positive attitude.

Nineveh's Repentance

Illustrating the truth of Hebrews 4:12, the living and active Word of God cuts like a double-edged sword, piercing the hearts of the Ninevites:

> Then the people of Nineveh believed in God; and they called a fast and put on sackcloth from the greatest to the least of them. When the word reached the king of Nineveh, he arose from his throne, laid aside his robe from him, covered himself with sackcloth and sat on the ashes. He issued a proclamation and it said, "In Nineveh by the decree of the king and his nobles:

Do not let man, beast, herd, or flock taste a thing. Do not let them eat or drink water. But both man and beast must be covered with sackcloth; and let men call on God earnestly that each may turn from his wicked way and from the violence which is in his hands. Who knows, God may turn and relent and withdraw His burning anger so that we will not perish."

When God saw their deeds, that they turned from their wicked way, then God relented concerning the calamity which He had declared He would bring upon them. And He did not do it. (Jonah 3:5–10)

Even the king of Nineveh, sitting in his palace, is touched by the carefully honed point of Jonah's message. At once, he abdicates his high position in the ominous face of God's wrath. He exchanges his throne and his royal robes for sackcloth and ashes. The repentance extends from "the greatest to the least"—from king to commoner, from man to beast. As a result of the people's repentance, God's wrath is averted. This benevolent mercy, as Joel states, is inherent to the Almighty's character:

> "Yet even now," declares the Lord,
> "Return to Me with all your heart,
> And with fasting, weeping and mourning;
> And rend your heart and not your garments."
> Now return to the Lord your God,
> For He is gracious and compassionate,
> Slow to anger, abounding in lovingkindness,
> And relenting of evil. (Joel 2:12–13)

Jonah's Reaction

The heat of God's anger is cooled by the tears of Nineveh's repentance. In His mercy, God issues the people a death-row reprieve from their slated execution. Jonah's reaction, however, is the complete opposite. Instead of responding in love like the prodigal son's compassionate father, Jonah reacts in a way that parallels the response of the critical older brother (see Luke 15:28).

> But it greatly displeased Jonah and he became angry. He prayed to the Lord and said, "Please Lord, was not this what I said while I was still in my own country? Therefore in order to forestall this I fled to Tarshish,

for I knew that You are a gracious and compassionate God, slow to anger and abundant in lovingkindness, and one who relents concerning calamity. "Therefore now, O Lord, please take my life from me, for death is better to me than life." The Lord said, "Do you have good reason to be angry?" (Jonah 4:1–4)

Notice carefully how God deals with the pouting prophet. No sermon. No rebuke. No argument. Just the barbed question that pricked like a fishhook into his heart: "Do you have good reason to be angry?"

It's possible to have all the right theology while having the wrong attitude and misguided motives. Notice how biblical Jonah's theology is: "I knew that You are a gracious and compassionate God, slow to anger and abundant in lovingkindness, and one who relents concerning calamity" (v. 2). Notice also his anger (v. 1). Right words, wrong heart attitude.

The parables in Luke 15 picture how our hearts should respond when a sinner repents. In each incident—the lost sheep (vv. 3–7), the lost coin (vv. 8–10), and the lost son (vv. 11–32)—what was lost was found, resulting in great joy (vv. 7, 10, 32). The father in the parable of the prodigal son illustrates the embracing, compassionate heart of God the Father toward a wayward child. In contrast, the critical older brother illustrates the indignant, self-righteous heart of the Pharisees and scribes (v. 2). Two portraits: a compassionate, accepting father, and a critical, angry brother.

This parable illustrates that you can dot every theological *i* and cross every doctrinal *t*, but still be far from God. As Jesus said to the hypocritical scribes and Pharisees:

> "'This people honors Me with their lips,
> But their heart is far away from Me.'" (Mark 7:6)

The prodigal son's brother lived under the same roof as the father, but his heart was miles away. How about you? How close is your heart to the Father's?

God's Rebuke

Stomping away in a huff, Jonah shook the city's dust off his feet and built a box seat on a hillside to view the city's fate:

> Then Jonah went out from the city and sat east of it. There he made a shelter for himself and sat

under it in the shade until he could see what would happen in the city. (Jonah 4:5)

The God of the sea who appointed the great fish to swallow Jonah is also the God of the earth who appoints a plant to shade him:

> So the Lord God appointed a plant and it grew up over Jonah to be a shade over his head to deliver him from his discomfort. And Jonah was extremely happy about the plant. (v. 6)

Note the great emotional response that this lower level of life brought to Jonah: "And Jonah was extremely happy about the plant." God uses this plant to sow an important object lesson in the hard soil of Jonah's heart:

> But God appointed a worm when dawn came the next day and it attacked the plant and it withered. When the sun came up God appointed a scorching east wind, and the sun beat down on Jonah's head so that he became faint and begged with all his soul to die, saying, "Death is better to me than life." (vv. 7–8)

God uses another part of His creation to act—this time a worm, and this time for destruction. Not only is Jonah's shade gone, but God also appoints a scorching east wind to descend upon him. As the sun beats down on the head of the prophet, his joy shrivels like the leaves of the plant. Longing for death, Jonah calls out to God in despair. But the Almighty provides no respite, only another pointed question:

> Then God said to Jonah, "Do you have good reason to be angry about the plant?" And he said, "I have good reason to be angry, even to death." (v. 9)

Jonah's answer flies in the face of God's patience, but He still calmly explains His reasons for letting the plant shrivel:

> Then the Lord said, "You had compassion on the plant for which you did not work and which you did not cause to grow, which came up overnight and perished overnight. Should I not have compassion on Nineveh, the great city in which there are more than 120,000 persons who do not know the difference between their right and left hand, as well as many animals?" (vv. 10–11)

God's sharp words pierce Jonah's soul and sting like salt in a wound. With a light hand but a sharp hoe, God cultivates the object lesson He planted in Jonah's heart. Essentially, God puts His arm around Jonah and says, "Let's talk about this concern you had for the plant, Jonah." God's argument could be summarized this way:

> "What did it really mean to you? Your attachment to it could not be very deep, for it was here one day and *gone the next*. Your concern was dictated by self-interest, not by a genuine love. You never had for it the devotion of the gardener. If you feel as badly as you do, what would you expect a gardener to feel like, who tended a plant and watched it grow only to see it wither and die, poor thing? And this is how I feel about Nineveh, only much more so. All those people, all those animals—I made them, I have cherished them all these years. Nineveh has cost me no end of effort, and they mean the world to me. Your pain is nothing to mine when I contemplate their destruction."[2]

With the object lesson finally deeply rooted in Jonah's heart, the embittered prophet stands silent before the court of heaven—a mute testimony to the truth of God's argument. And thus we leave Jonah, never to hear his voice in the Scriptures again. We hope that God's moving demonstration of mercy changed Jonah's heart and motivated him to keep sharing the Word of God with others.

Living Insights

For most of this story, Jonah's value scale was unbalanced and his vision myopic. He selfishly ran from God to avoid sharing His message, and an insignificant, soulless plant meant more to him than all the people of Nineveh combined. Jonah demonstrated repeatedly that deep down he was more concerned about *Jonah* than he was about *Nineveh*.

What's the main lesson that your life teaches? Are you more concerned with building shelters and raising plants—more concerned

---

2. Leslie C. Allen, *The Books of Joel, Obadiah, Jonah, and Micah*, a volume of the *International Commentary on the Old Testament* (Grand Rapids, Mich.: William B. Eerdmans Publishing Co., 1976), p. 221.

about creature comforts and selfish living—than the deep spiritual needs of people?

On a one-to-ten scale—one being your concern for your own physical comfort and ten being your concern for the spiritual needs of others—how would you evaluate yourself, and why?

_____

_____

_____

_____

What needs to take place in your life to increase your care and concern for others? Read Philippians 2:3–8 for some perspective.

_____

_____

_____

_____

What do you feel is your "Nineveh"? What ministries, goals, and tasks has God gifted and called you to do?

_____

_____

_____

_____

Are there some distractions in your life that need to be removed so you can better minister to the people in your Nineveh? If so, what are they?

_____

_____

_____

_____

_____

The pain that Jonah and some of our other Old Testament characters brought on themselves illustrates that when we deliberately sin and disobey God's orders, we reap tragic consequences. In contrast, we've learned from others that we can live a victorious, abundant, peace-filled life when we choose to sacrifice ourselves to put God first and obey His commands. Though our circumstances will not be perfect until we enter eternity, we can have spiritual joy when we know we're in the center of the Lord's will.

 Questions for Group Discussion

1. If you could use three words to describe Jonah, what would they be?

2. Do you think Jonah's character and attitudes changed as a result of his experience in Nineveh? If so, why? If not, why not?

3. If you could use three words to describe yourself currently, what would they be?

4. If you could choose three attributes that you would like to have when you come to the end of your life, what would they be? How can you go about cultivating these characteristics?

5. Has God ever used an object lesson to get your attention? If so, what was it, and how did it work?

6. Which of the Old Testament characters we've studied (Samson, Abigail, Absalom, Rehoboam, Naaman, Gehazi, Jabez, Uzziah, Esther, Jonah) are you most like? Why?

BOOKS FOR
PROBING FURTHER

In his essay *Reflections in Westminster Abbey*, seventeenth-century writer Joseph Addison records his thoughts about a stroll through the church and burial place of Britain's famous.

> When I look upon the tombs of the great, every emotion of envy dies in me. When I read the epitaphs of the beautiful, every inordinate desire goes out. When I meet with the grief of parents upon a tombstone, my heart melts with compassion. When I see the tomb of the parents themselves, I consider the vanity of grieving for those whom we must quickly follow. When I see kings lying by those who deposed them, when I consider rival wits placed side by side, or the holy men that divided the world with their contests and disputes, I reflect with sorrow and astonishment on the little competitions, factions, and debates of mankind. When I read the several dates of the tombs, of some that died yesterday, and some six hundred years ago, I consider that great day when we shall all of us be contemporaries, and make our appearance together.[1]

We hope that you've benefited from your walk through the lives of these Old Testament characters. Like each of us, these people struggled through trials and suffered as a result of their sins, but their stories still resonate with biblical principles and God's message of redemption. Listed below are several books that will help you in your further study of the characters and issues addressed in this guide.

Arterburn, Stephen, Fred Stoecker with Mike Yorkey. *Every Man's Battle: Winning the War on Sexual Temptation One Victory at a Time*. Colorado Springs, Colo.: WaterBrook Press, 2000.

Blaiklock, E. M. *Today's Handbook of Bible Characters*. Minneapolis, Minn.: Bethany House Publishers, 1987.

---

1. As quoted in *The Original McGuffey's: The Fourth Eclectic Reader*, ed. Jean Morton (Milford, Mich.: Mott Media, 1982), pp. 401–402.

Dyer, Charles and Gene Merrill. *The Old Testament Explorer: Discovering the Essence, Background, and Meaning of Every Book in the Old Testament.* Nashville, Tenn.: Word Publishing, 2001.

Ethridge, Shannon. *Every Woman's Battle: Discovering God's Plan for Sexual and Emotional Fulfillment.* Colorado Springs, Colo.: Water-Brook Press, 2003.

Maxwell, John C. *Running with the Giants: What Old Testament Heroes Want You to Know about Life and Leadership.* New York, N.Y.: Warner Books, 2002.

Moore, Beth. *When Godly People Do Ungodly Things: Finding Authentic Restoration in the Age of Seduction.* Nashville, Tenn.: Broadman and Holman Publishers, 2002.

————. *Praying God's Word: Breaking Free from Spiritual Strongholds.* Nashville, Tenn.: Broadman and Holman Publishers, 2000.

Osbeck, Kenneth W. *52 Bible Characters Dramatized: Easy-to-Use Monologues for All Occasions.* Grand Rapids, Mich.: Kregel Publications, 1996.

Scazzero, Peter. *Old Testament Characters: 12 Studies for Individuals or Groups.* Downers Grove, Ill.: InterVarsity Press, 2000.

Spangler, Ann and Robert D. Wolgemuth. *Men of the Bible: A One-Year Devotional Study of Men in Scripture.* Grand Rapids, Mich.: Zondervan Publishing House, 2002.

Spangler, Ann and Jean E. Syswerda. *Women of the Bible: A One-Year Devotional Study of Women in Scripture.* Grand Rapids, Mich.: Zondervan Publishing House, 1999.

Wiersbe, Warren W. *Classic Sermons on Lesser Known Bible Characters.* Grand Rapids, Mich.: Kregel Publications, 2000.

Some of these books may be out of print and available only through a library. For those currently available, please contact your local Christian bookstore or online resource. Many books by Charles R. Swindoll may be obtained through Insight for Living. IFL also offers some books by other authors. Please note the ordering information that follows and contact the office that serves you.

Ordering Information

Old Testament Characters

If you would like to order additional Bible study guides, purchase the audiocassette series that accompanies this guide, or request our product catalogs, please contact the office that serves you.

United States and International Locations:

Insight for Living
Post Office Box 269000
Plano, TX 75026-9000
1-800-772-8888, 24 hours a day, seven days a week (U.S. contacts)
International constituents may contact the U.S. office through mail queries.

Canada:

Insight for Living Ministries
Post Office Box 2510
Vancouver, BC, Canada V6B 3W7
1-800-663-7639, 24 hours a day, seven days a week
info@insightcanada.org

Australia:

Insight for Living, Inc.
Suite 4, 43 Railway Rd.
Blackburn, VIC 3130, AUSTRALIA
Toll-free 1800 772 888 or (03) 9877-4277, 9:00 A.M. to 5:00 P.M., Monday through Friday
info@aus.insight.org

Internet:

www.insight.org

Bible Study Guide Subscription Program

Bible study guide subscriptions are available. Please call or write the office nearest you to find out how you can receive our Bible study guides on a regular basis.